Welcome to Bed & Breakfast Washington

Quimper Inn, Port Townsend

Welcome to Bed & Breakfast Washington

A Guide to the Guest Houses of Washington

Photography by Kay Green
Text by Lewis Green

New Horizons Publishers
Seattle

Published by New Horizons Publishers
Seattle, Washington

Library of Congress Catalog
Number: 83-63518

ISBN: 0-915325-00-4

Printed by Toppan Printing Co., Ltd.
Tokyo, Japan

Editor: Lewis Green

Editorial assistant: Brenda Burton

Design and production:
Ed Marquand Communication Design

Typesetting: Magna Color Press

To Richard and Kathy Louv
who gifted us
with inspiration and good karma.

Contents

Starrett House Inn, Port Townsend

A Journey Through Washington's Bed & Breakfast Homes

We left the safety of our Seattle apartment at 5 a.m. on a foggy Tuesday to begin the first trek of our 10-week bed and breakfast adventure. Even the birds were still asleep as we sneaked down our driveway and headed toward Highway 2, which would lead us to our first stop in the Bavarian village of Leavenworth.

Even though we were slightly familiar with bed and breakfast European style and the inns of New England, Kay and I really weren't sure what to expect from Washington's bed and breakfast industry.

We had talked with both Pacific Bed & Breakfast and Travellers', the two largest reservation services in the state, so we had an idea what we would find. But, as it turned out, we were in for quite a surprise.

Even though Irmgard (Pacific) and Jean (Travellers') had spent many hours with us explaining the nature of bed and breakfast, it was necessary for us to experience it firsthand before our imperfect perceptions were dispelled.

First, rates in the state of Washington range from $16 a night to $110 a night. The price of a room, or a house in the case of the $110 rate, is directly related to decor and location. Service has nothing to do with the price of lodging. The quality of the service will nearly always be superior to anything you will find in a hotel or motel.

Second, lodging runs the gamut of a tiny room that is furnished practically to an award-winning house that sits on a cliff and overlooks Admiralty Inlet. Cleanliness and safety are not a factor in pricing. All the homes that we visited were very clean. Most were equipped with smoke alarms, and some had sprinkler systems and/or fire extinguishers.

It can also be said that the rates have nothing to do with either the quality or quantity of the food. Breakfast usually includes some home-baked specialties and is usually more than most people can eat. All of the homes in our book include breakfast in their rates, but in some instances it is optional and in some instances it is cook-your-own. Breakfast ranges from continental to full. When booking a reservation, you should inquire as to what the breakfast includes and if it is optional.

The first stop on our adventure made us keenly aware of much of what I have just told you.

As we came over the mountains and eyed Leavenworth, our excitement reached a fever pitch. We wondered what our first visit would have in store for us. What would the house look like?

We drove up the long, winding unpaved driveway to Brown's Farm. As we turned the last corner, we saw their sign. Then we spotted their home. To us it was a beautiful sight and a wonderful relief.

Nestled on the side of a mountain amid a verdant forest was Brown's Farm – a log cabin that fit perfectly within its surroundings. It was our first clue that there really is a bed and breakfast home for every traveller. And it was also our first realization that not every bed and breakfast home will suit every traveller's needs. Bed and breakfast is not like the endless parade of look-alike motels and hotels. We were beginning to learn that every home is different and will appeal to different kinds of people. Next we learned something about bed and breakfast hosts.

Wendi Brown greeted us at the door as if we were friends. She welcomed us into the living room where we met Steve. Before we had a chance to think about our need for a hot beverage, Wendi was serving us tea.

The Browns are typical of the hosts and hostesses whom we met on our visits to Washington's bed and breakfast homes. Warm, friendly, and caring people are the rule and

Brown's Farm, Leavenworth

not the exception. Although it would be dishonest to say that all the people we met were as friendly as the Browns, we can assure you that the proprietors of Washington's homes will treat you cordially and with respect.

That night we enjoyed our first night's sleep in a Washington bed and breakfast home. Kay and I spent the evening at the farm and we loved it. It was quiet and restful, which seems to be the trademark of most of the homes we visited.

Leavenworth is a microcosm of bed and breakfast Washington. In that respect it is like Whidbey Island. The diverse nature of bed and breakfast is apparent in both of these areas.

After our visit to Brown's Farm, we continued our tour of Leavenworth. The next home we visited was a ranch-style house, followed by our visit to Haus Rohrbach, a large Bavarian inn with a swimming pool, and then followed by a stop at the elegant Edel Haus.

Our trip to Leavenworth was both educational and fun. We learned a great deal about bed and breakfast in a short period of time. The people we met made it fun for us.

As we left Leavenworth and made our way toward Chelan, we felt good about the project and relieved that our book would not be aimed at any one class or segment of society. The diverse nature of bed and breakfast had really hit home with us. And as we continued our adventure, we were constantly reminded of bed and breakfast's wide range of appeal.

From the Cascade Mountains, to the islands of the Sound, and on to the mansions of Seattle and Port Townsend, we discovered something for everyone's tastes. And so will you if you look carefully.

Log cabins, Victorian and

Mercer Island home

Penn Cove Inn, Coupeville

Georgian mansions, cozy rooms in houses originally built for sea captains, upstairs and downstairs apartments, rooms with spectacular views, and simple homey rooms are all on Washington's bed and breakfast menu.

Furnishings range from the old to the new, country pine antique to contemporary chrome, Queen Anne to Baroque, European to Middle Eastern, and worn to regal.

Service is as diverse as the decor and ambiance. Again there is something for everyone.

In the mountains guests can find hosts and hostesses who will provide them with information about hiking and skiing. Visitors may also receive free cross-country ski instruction. They may even be provided with skis or snowshoes.

On the Sound visitors may find themselves on a sailing voyage arranged by their host. They may be offered the use of a small boat for the day. Information about where to find the best fishing in the area or what to look for while walking the beaches is often readily available.

While in the urban areas, guests may be met at the airport or ferry terminal by their host, who is graciously providing them with free transportation. Visitors may also receive an auto-tour of the city or be provided with privy information about the host's favorite restaurant or the hottest ticket in town.

Based upon our experiences, we have decided to make all of the descriptions in our book as appealing as possible without sacrificing honesty. We consciously chose not to rate the homes which are listed in this book. We believe that every home has something to offer. We don't wish to discourage anyone from finding their own little piece of nirvana.

When you are reading the descriptions, you should keep this firmly in mind. Every home we visited was unique. We found something to love in each one. The descriptions reflect this attitude.

But remember that tastes vary greatly. Therefore, when selecting your lodging, you must choose based upon your personal preferences. We encourage you to read the descriptions with a discriminating eye and to use the photographs to help you with your selections.

Then we suggest that you call the home or homes (or agency) that you have chosen and ask some pertinent questions. Try to get a real feel for the environment. Do the proprietors allow smoking in their guest rooms?

Em's, Chelan

The Saratoga Inn, Langley

Countryman's, Snohomish

Can you bring along your children or your pets? We discovered that most homes do not permit smoking, children, or pets, but there are exceptions. Does it seem to you that you are going to like the hosts and enjoy staying with them? This last point is very important because you will probably be spending some time with the host or hostess.

We strongly recommend all the homes we visited. However, some of the homes that appear in this book were not visited by us. Those are clearly marked by a line that reads, "Description Provided By Agency or Host." We assume that these homes have the same high standards as the ones we visited, but we cannot personally recommend them to you.

The one thing that I will guarantee you is that every visit to a different bed and breakfast home will be unique. Expect the unexpected and prepare yourself to be pampered.

As you read through *Bed & Breakfast Washington,* I hope you find many homes that interest you. But whether you enjoy your visit to a bed and breakfast home depends mostly on how carefully you choose your destination.

Let me remind you once again that not every home is for every traveller. And if you have never experienced the adventure of travelling the bed and breakfast way, keep in mind that you will not be staying in the sterile environment that you may have become used to while staying in motels and hotels.

The Captain's House, Bainbridge Island

You will be a paying guest in someone's private home. Every home will be different and every room in every home will be different. The rules are made by the hosts to make your stay as enjoyable as possible.

We hope you will write us to let us know about your bed and breakfast experiences. If you have any suggestions for the improvement of this book, please let us know. Also, if you own a bed and breakfast home in Washington and were not included in this edition but would like to be in the next edition, please contact us. Kay and I can be reached at our home address, which is 737 10th Avenue East, Seattle, WA 98102. Have fun!

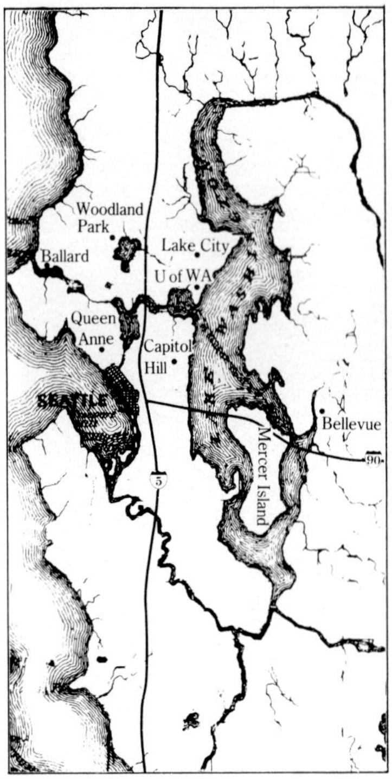

Buildings are soaring skyward and freeways are becoming more crowded, still Seattle and its neighboring communities remain beautiful livable cities where people come first and retain the distinction of being more important than concrete and steel.

Buses and ferries are clean and run on schedule; Freeway Park is a quiet touch of greenery blossoming where only buildings once grew tall; the waterfront is safe, clean, and a haven for tourists; Pike Place Market is alive with energy and the sounds of a healthy and friendly city echo throughout its stalls; flowers dot the city's landscape and trees are left untouched to grow in peace; and Seattle's neighboring bedroom communities are a maze of tranquil subdivisions.

Seattle's downtown business and shopping areas perk with excitement. You will have no trouble filling days with interesting and fun excursions to the myriad of attractions served on a banquet buffet of recreation and entertainment.

And there is water everywhere. There are more boats per capita in Seattle (one out of every six Seattleites owns a boat of 16 feet or more) than any other city in the United States.

Surrounding Greater Seattle, the Cascade and Olympic Mountains look on as gentle reminders that escape to a lush forest or a blue crystalline mountain lake is just out the door, around the corner, and down the street.

The Seattle Center

One of the area's guidebooks calls the Seattle Center the city's hub of recreation, culture, and entertainment. This is an apt description.

There is no admission to this 74-acre park that once served as the location for the 1962 World's Fair, which was one of the few World's Fairs to pay its own way.

For the spirited there is Fun Forest, a carnival of rides and games. If your children are with you (or if you're a child at heart), plan to spend a lot of time here.

For those of you who are "young" enough to remember Mr. Wizard and his message that science is fun, be sure to visit the Pacific Science Center.

The Space Needle literally tops the list of other attractions at the Center, which includes the Laserium, the Center House, Coliseum, Opera House, Bagley Wright Theatre, Playhouse, Arena, Mural Amphitheater, and the Seattle Art Museum Pavilion.

Pike Place Market

Throughout the year thousands of visitors come to sample the wares of the fresh fruit and vegetable sellers, fish and meat merchants, as well as the artists and craftsmen who occupy the stalls of this tiny city within a city.

Alongside the stall-keepers are antique stores, handicraft shops, art galleries, restaurants, and pubs.

The Waterfront

Shops, restaurants, and even a park make up Seattle's "recreational" waterfront that stretches from the Alaska Ferry dock at Pier 48 to a two-story warehouse filled with more than 40 shops at Pier 70.

Pioneer Square

Galleries, boutiques, restaurants, bookstores, antique stores, and buildings that date back to circa 1890 make up this 20-square-block area that was the birthplace of Seattle. Because of the great fire of 1889, which consumed the area's wooden structures, a new city of brick was built. Streets were raised, some by as much as 18 feet, and an "underground city" evolved. Today it is a tourist attraction.

Seattle's Neighbors and Neighborhoods

Ballard

With the exception of Interstate 5, perhaps the busiest highway in the city is located in Ballard. Known locally as the Ballard Locks (but officially as the Hiram M. Chittenden Locks), this water-escalator connects freshwater Lake Union and Lake Washington with salty Puget Sound. Picknickers spend hours watching everything from canoes to ocean-going vessels passing through.

Ballard is a quiet residential Nordic community that is home to the Nordic Heritage Museum, the Carl S. English Memorial Gardens, the Fisherman's Terminal, Shilshole Bay Marina, Golden Gardens Park, and the Ballard Avenue Historical District.

Bellevue

This is Washington's fourth largest city. It is located on the east side of Lake Washington about 20 minutes from downtown Seattle.

Bellevue is a community composed of many Northwest-style homes that are perched on roomy wooded lots. It is a fast-growing city that is developing its own identity and is leaving behind the trademark of suburbia. Still, it is charming and carries proudly the veil of Northwest wooded ambiance.

Bellevue has a strong retail center that includes more than 20 shopping centers. It also boasts a fine array of cultural attractions including the Bellevue Philharmonic Orchestra and the Bellevue Art Museum.

Capitol Hill

This hilltop neighborhood is for the young at heart, mind, and spirit. Its residents, young and old, artist and professional, display a certain zest for life that is inescapable to all around them. It is the one neighborhood in Seattle that encourages a bohemian attitude and flourishes because of it rather than in spite of it.

Capitol Hill is the home of Volunteer Park, the Seattle Art Museum, the Conservatory, and some of the finest old mansions anywhere. Its residential neighborhoods are clean, green, and quiet.

Its main street, Broadway, is a center for boutiques. Night life along this busy street is upbeat. Its spirit is characterized by the bronze "dancing feet" that visitors will discover as they walk along the sidewalk.

Green Lake

Green Lake, which is just north of Woodland Park Zoo, is a lovely neighborhood that serves as a giant playground for the city. It is a haven for joggers, roller skaters, sunbathers, fishermen, and bike riders. In the summer there are crew and boat races on the lake.

Lake City

Located about ten minutes north of downtown, this area gives visitors an opportunity to be far from the hustle and bustle of downtown yet within easy driving distance.

Mercer Island

Quiet residential neighborhoods dot this picturesque island that is only minutes from downtown Seattle. It offers perhaps the best opportunity for visitors to view the contemporary style of Northwest residential living.

Queen Anne

Queen Anne is really two neighborhoods rolled into one. Lower Queen Anne borders the Seattle Center and is alive with people having fun.

As one travels up the hill, the area becomes quiet and dignified. Lovely homes alongside apartments and condominiums dot the hillsides and hilltop. Tiny parks provide visitors with tranquil settings for reading a good book or just observing the city life below.

Several very good restaurants can be found on lower Queen Anne. Spectacular views of the mountains and Puget Sound are available from atop the hill.

University District

Obviously the University of Washington holds center stage in this neighborhood. Its facilities and activities dominate the entire area. Visitors are welcome to tour the spacious and beautiful campus as well as enjoy the many cultural, sports, and other activities the University offers.

Wallingford

This neighborhood is only five minutes from the University District and the downtown area. It has a number of small shops and fine restaurants as well as the Guild 45th, one of the finest theaters in town.

Woodland Park

This is not a neighborhood at all. It is a park that boasts one of the finest zoos in the United States. A quiet residential neighborhood borders the park.

POINTS OF INTEREST

Arboretum University of Washington, 543-8800
Ballard Locks 783-7001
Discovery Park 625-4636
Freeway Park between Boren and Sixth Avenues and Hubble and Spring Streets
Frye Art Museum 622-9250
Henry Art Gallery University of Washington, 543-2280
Monorail Westlake Mall to Seattle Center, 625-4234
Pacific Science Center 625-9333
Pike Place Market First Avenue and Pike, 625-4762
Pioneer Square south of downtown
Seattle Art Museum Volunteer Park, 447-4710
Seattle Center 74-acre urban park, 625-4234
Seattle Marine Aquarium Pier 59, 625-4357
Space Needle 447-3100
Woodland Park Zoo 789-7919

PERFORMING ARTS

Pacific Northwest Ballet	447-4751
Paramount	624-5772
Seattle Opera Association	447-4700
Seattle Symphony . . .	447-4746

PHONE NUMBERS

British Columbia Tourism	206 623-5937
Convention and Visitors Bureau	206 447-7273
Customs	206 442-4678
Emergencies	911
Highway Patrol . .	206 455-7700
Jackson International Airport	206 433-5218
Library Quick Information	206 625-2665
Metro Transit System	206 447-4800
Seattle Chamber of Commerce	206 447-7200
Seattle Parks and Recreation	206 625-4671
Washington State Ferries	206 464-6400 or 1 800 542-0810

ADDRESSES

Seattle-King County Visitors Bureau
1815 Seventh Avenue
Seattle, WA 98101

Seattle Parks and Recreation
5201 Green Lake Way North
Seattle, WA 98103

CHAMBERED NAUTILUS

5005 22nd Avenue N.E.
Seattle, WA
98105
206 522-2536

Kate and Deborah have created an atmosphere that will allow their guests to feel as cozy and comfortable in their surroundings as the little sea creature for which the home was named. Located in the heart of Seattle's University District in a quiet residential neighborhood, the home is within a short distance of Seattle's theaters, restaurants, and shopping areas. Both Kate and Deborah like to share information about Seattle with their guests. The home has six bedrooms that share three bathrooms. Four of the bedrooms have porches where guests can practice the art of relaxation. Kate, a gourmet baker, prepares breakfast. Before breakfast guests may wish to view the art that is hanging on the gallery wall in the living room, or they may prefer to build up their appetites by joining Deborah and Keri, the house Samoyed, for a morning run. Rates are $40 to $60 for a double and reservations are suggested.

QUEEN ANNE

Seattle, WA
Pacific: 206 784-0539

Guests will be treated to a home within a home when they stay in this spacious upstairs apartment. Large windows surround the apartment on three sides, providing panoramic views of the city and the snow-crested mountains. The home's owner, Peggy, has comfortably furnished the large living room. The kitchen is completely equipped. Peggy keeps it well-stocked with food for her guests, who are free to prepare their own breakfast. The home is located within a few minutes of downtown. When guests return from an exciting evening in the city, they may wish to take advantage of the beautiful private sauna that has been built into their accommodations and beckons them to ease back and relax. Guests may also enjoy sunbathing on the private deck. Rates are $30 (single) to $40 (double) and reservations are required.

QUEEN ANNE

Seattle, WA
Pacific: 206 784-0539

Margaret enjoyed her overnight stays at European bed and breakfasts so much that she decided to import this style of lodging into her own home. She feels it gives visitors an opportunity to be among friends immediately in an otherwise unfamiliar city. Her home is conveniently close to downtown and is within easy walking distance of a bus stop. Her downstairs guest room is cozy, comfortably furnished, and has its own private half-bath. Guests share the full bathroom with their hostess. Margaret invites her guests to make themselves at home and to feel free to use the entire home. Breakfast is served on beautiful hand-painted Hadley dishes in a little nook that has a view of the Cascade Mountains and Lake Washington. On those lazy days of summer, guests will enjoy lounging on the deck or in the manicured yard. Rates are $20 (single) to $30 (double) and reservations are required.

QUEEN ANNE

Seattle, WA
Pacific: 206 784-0539
Travellers': 206 232-2345

Stand at the windows of this upstairs apartment-like guest room and gaze at the spectacular panorama before you. It's as if a grand and beautiful painting had been created just for you. Your eyes are drawn first to the grandeur of Mt. Rainier and the Cascade Mountains, then move slowly to the impressive downtown Seattle skyline standing guard over Puget Sound. Finally, they come to the snowcapped Olympic Mountain range. After your eyes have feasted on this glorious view of Washington, Laine and Hank invite you to sunbathe on their private patio, or take a quiet walk through Hank's vegetable garden. Rates are $40 to $45 for a double and reservations are required.

QUEEN ANNE

Seattle, WA
Pacific: 206 784-0539
Travellers': 206 232-2345

Breathtaking views of Puget Sound and the Olympic Mountains are the trademark of this lovely home that is centrally located. Mary and Chuck have decorated their home with fun in mind and hope guests will enjoy the many art pieces, collector's items, teddy bears, and Chuck's private collection of scales. Both upstairs guest rooms are well-stocked with books and have desks. One of the rooms is furnished with a double and a twin bed. It has its own private deck. Guests enter the downstairs deck through a cozy sun room. The downstairs living room is furnished comfortably and has a fireplace. Breakfast is served on an antique table in the dining room and may include home-baked goodies, homemade granola, and fresh fruit. Rates are $25 (single) to $40 (double) and reservations are required.

QUEEN ANNE

Seattle, WA
Pacific: 206 784-0539

Elsa wants her guests to make themselves right at home in this large city apartment that is located only five minutes from Seattle Center and provides easy access to all the sights and activities of the city. Guests are welcome to enjoy the spacious living room. They may feel like warming themselves in front of the fireplace while reading a good book. Great views of the city and Puget Sound can be appreciated from the living room, the large guest room, and the balcony. A restful night's sleep is guaranteed in the quiet guest room that is attractively furnished and includes a brass bed. A private bathroom is provided for guests. Elsa makes it easy for guests to enjoy their favorite midnight snack by encouraging them to store their treats in the kitchen. Breakfast is served in either the formal dining room or, in warm weather, on the balcony. Rates are $26 (single) to $35 (double) and reservations are required.

GALER PLACE

318 West Galer Street
Seattle, WA
98119
206 282-5339

A south Queen Anne Hill location in a quiet residential neighborhood is the setting for this 1906 home that captures the feeling of turn-of-the-century living in a fanciful bed and breakfast guest house. The tranquil environment allows time for guests to share an afternoon cup of tea, discuss out-of-the-way cafes, or take a soothing dip in the hot tub. Later in the evening as the bright lights of the city begin to beckon, guests will welcome the convenience of being just a short jaunt from Seattle Center, fine restaurants, exciting theater, and downtown Seattle. Visitors are encouraged to walk to several nearby viewpoints that provide breathtaking looks at both the city skyline and the mountains. The upstairs guest rooms share a bathroom. Guests are welcome downstairs to enjoy the cozy parlor. A continental breakfast is served in the dining room. Rates are $35 to $45 for a double and reservations are suggested.

THE WILLIAMS HOUSE

1505 Fourth Avenue North
Seattle, WA
98109
206 285-0810

Susan, Doug, and Danielle, their beautiful baby girl, shower their guests with the gift of warmth and friendliness as they welcome them into this large family home. The Williams House is a little retreat in the city that combines easy city access and old-world Victorian comfort. And for those who wish to hold a warm and cuddly bundle of joy, Danielle is happy to cooperate. Guests will quickly discover that Susan and Doug wish to make their home their visitors' home. They are eager to share information about places to go and things to see and do in Seattle and the Puget Sound area. For those who enjoy the pleasure of a quiet walk, the neighborhood is both scenic and friendly. And for the more athletic types, a cinder track, public swimming pool, and YMCA facilities are nearby. The home is also available for weddings, receptions, and small group meetings. The guest rooms share two large bathrooms and rates are $32 (single) to $55 (double). Reservations are suggested.

MERCER ISLAND

Mercer Island, WA
BABS: 206 733-8642

The location of this home provides guests with easy access to the interstate, downtown Seattle, and the airport. It is also a short distance from public swimming, tennis courts, and Lake Washington. Marge and Dick are interested in gardening, antique furniture, antique cars, and natural foods. In fact, Marge teaches classes on how to cook natural foods. One bedroom is furnished with a queen-size bed, the other with a twin bed. Both rooms share a bathroom. Breakfast is served in the dining room or, weather permitting, on the patio. Rates are $17.50 (single) to $25 (double) and reservations are required. Description Provided By Agency.

MERCER ISLAND

Mercer Island, WA
Travellers': 206 232-2345

Immediately upon entering this lovely home you have the sense that you are with folks who have been your friends for a long time. Mary and Bill are warm, sincere, and caring people who make their guests feel right at home. Whether it's a friendly but spirited game of bridge in the evening, playing a piano duet with Mary, or just sitting in the kitchen and sipping the day's first cup of coffee while Mary and Bill prepare breakfast, guests will appreciate the time they spend with these fine people. Both guest rooms are quiet, comfortable, and share a large bathroom. Guests are given their own key for their convenience. They are encouraged to enjoy the entire home and are welcome to use the laundry room. Breakfast is served either in the formal dining room or, when weather permits, on the patio. The home is conveniently located to Seattle and the airport. Rates are $30 to $40 for a double and reservations are required.

MERCER ISLAND

Mercer Island, WA
Pacific: 206 784-0539
Travellers': 206 232-2345

There is no threat of flashing neon signs disturbing guests' sleep in this private home that is located in a wooded area of a quiet residential neighborhood. The entire downstairs serves as guest accommodations. The bedroom has a queen-size bed, a small sitting area, and tall windows that make it light and airy. The large sitting room is comfortably furnished and has a wood stove, a color television, and a large library of books and magazines. A private deck that overlooks the East Channel is the perfect place for lounging. In the morning guests are awakened by the smell of fresh ground coffee filtering down the stairs. Your hostess, Anne, awaits in the formal dining room for her guests to be seated to a breakfast of fresh fruit, homemade muffins, juice, and a delicious entree. Rates are $30 (single) to $40 (double) and reservations are required.

MERCER ISLAND

Mercer Island, WA
Pacific: 206 784-0539
Travellers': 206 232-2345

Elegance, charm, and grace are the trademarks of this beautiful home and its charming hostess, Shirley. When guests enter their downstairs guest room, they will feel as if they have stepped into a fantasy world fit for royalty. As they sip their sherry, their eyes will take a splendid voyage that previously had been reserved only for their imaginations. Each guest room is unique. In one, guests will dream of a bygone era as they snuggle beneath the down comforter that keeps them warm in their canopy bed. Both rooms have distinctive furniture and are tastefully decorated. A private sitting room separates the guest rooms and offers color television, a small refrigerator, and a telescope for star gazing. Breakfast is served in the formal dining room beneath a crystal chandelier which once hung from the ceiling of a Paris theater. Rates are $45 for a double and reservations are required.

MERCER ISLAND

Mercer Island, WA
Travellers': 206 232-2345

This contemporary home is located only five minutes from the interstate but provides guests with the seclusion and quiet atmosphere of a home in the country. Nestled in a wooded area on a bluff, the home offers the convenience of nearby shopping and is only fifteen minutes from downtown Seattle. Partial views of Lake Washington, Mt. Baker, and the Cascade Mountains are available from the guest room, living room, deck, and dining room. The upstairs accommodations include a comfortable bedroom with a writing table and chairs, a sitting room complete with a wood stove and comfortable sofa, and a private bathroom that has a skylight directly above the vanity. Guests are also invited to relax in the downstairs living room or lounge on the deck. The hostess of this lovely home has travelled a great deal and is very knowledgeable about bed and breakfast. She offers a casual and informal at-home atmosphere. Rates are $25 (single) to $40 (double) and reservations are required.

CAPITOL HILL

Seattle, WA
Pacific: 206 784-0539
Travellers': 206 232-2345

The elegance and charm of this home and its hostess, Mildred, are a joy to behold. Guests from every corner of the world have had the pleasure of spending valuable time with this warm and gracious hostess. Upon arriving, Mildred's guests are greeted at the front door and welcomed into her living room to sit in front of the fire and share a refreshment while they become acquainted. The home is located directly across the street from Volunteer Park and is within a short walk of the Seattle Art Museum and the Conservatory. The upstairs guest rooms are bathed in sunlight. Guests share a large bathroom that is as special and unique as the rest of the house. A half-bath is also available. In the morning guests awaken to a soft knock on their door. Mildred bids them good morning, bringing them their morning coffee or juice. The rates are $30 (single) to $35 (double) and reservations are required.

CAPITOL HILL

Seattle, WA
Pacific: 206 784-0539
Travellers': 206 232-2345

Mary is the cordial and outgoing hostess of this beautiful brick home that is conveniently located within a short distance of downtown Seattle, the University District, and the Seattle Art Museum. It is on a very quiet street in a residential neighborhood. Guests are given their own key to use while they are visiting and are welcome to make themselves at home in the entire house. There are two upstairs guest rooms that share a bathroom. The larger room has twin beds and a cozy dressing room. When guests are not out taking walking tours of the city, they may wish to spend some time in Mary's living room, which is comfortably furnished with Queen Anne and Baroque furniture and is adorned with art from Europe. Breakfast is served in the formal dining room and rates are $25 (single) to $35 (double). Reservations are required.

CAPITOL HILL

Seattle, WA
Pacific: 206 784-0539

Stately sycamore trees surround this lovely turn-of-the-century home which is located in a quiet residential neighborhood. It is within easy walking distance of Volunteer Park, the Conservatory, the Art Museum, and, for the more athletic types, tennis courts. The guest rooms are comfortable and have private bathrooms. The elegant living room is furnished with antiques and several extraordinary family heirlooms. Guests are invited to play the baby grand piano. A fireplace with an Alaskan marble face helps to warm the room. Joyce and Henry are flexible and wish to meet the needs of their guests by providing comfort and service. A tasty Pacific Northwest breakfast is prepared by Joyce and is served in the formal dining room. There is private parking available for guests. Rates are $27 (single) to $40 (double) and reservations are required.

CAPITOL HILL

Seattle, WA
Travellers': 206 232-2345

Rod and Karen wish to develop a rapport with their guests, who often become friends. On a recent visit to Lyon, France, Rod and Karen took the time to visit their very first guest. Karen speaks fluent French. She is also a flutist and teaches gourmet cooking. Rod is responsible for much of the recent renovation of their 1907 home. The upstairs guest room is furnished with antiques and shares a bathroom. Much of the home is adorned with family heirlooms. Guests are welcome to relax in the living room, which has a fireplace. Breakfast is served in the dining room. This home is located only one block from Broadway, one of the most exciting and alluring streets in the city, yet is in a very quiet neighborhood. Guests are just ten minutes from downtown and the University District. Rates are $30 (single) to $35 (double) and reservations are required.

CAPITOL HILL

Seattle, WA
Pacific: 206 784-0539

When guests walk into this north Capitol Hill home, they can almost taste the European flavor of the decor. Liliane is from Germany, speaks English, German, and French, and has successfully created an environment that is essentially European. The guest rooms are located upstairs and share a full bathroom. One room has a king-size bed, a color television, a lovely antique desk, and a partial view of Lake Washington and the Cascade Mountains. Guests are welcome to lounge in the living room and enjoy the peacefulness of this quiet residential neighborhood, or they may prefer to investigate the University District, several nearby parks, the Seattle Art Museum, or the University of Washington Arboretum. Rates are $25 (single) to $40 (double) and reservations are required.

INTERLAKEN BED & BREAKFAST

2149 East Interlaken
Boulevard
Seattle, WA
98112
206 323-0760

Genie and Gary Hagar have created an authentic bed and breakfast experience in the European tradition. They have two small children, David and Stefan, and guests will experience a family environment while staying in the home. Both Genie and Gary are sensitive to the needs of their guests and attempt to strike a balance between respecting their guests' privacy and providing companionship and personal attention. The home is located in a scenic wooded area near the University of Washington. It is within walking distance of the University, museums, parks, libraries, tennis courts, and biking trails. Accommodations are on the second floor of the home and include two adjoining bedrooms which are separated by a half-bath. Children are welcome and a crib is available for the little ones. Rates are $25 (single) to $35 (double) and reservations are suggested.

WALLINGFORD

Seattle, WA
Pacific: 206 784-0539

Audrey is the gracious hostess of this centrally located Colonial-style home. Guests will enjoy meeting this lovely lady who is a former librarian and who has an avid interest in art. Both guest accommodations are upstairs and share a bathroom. The master suite is large and opens out onto a private sun deck that is a great place to lounge. It offers a partial view of the Olympic Mountains. Furnishings include a desk, a double bed, and a twin bed. The suite also has an adjoining dressing room. A special feature upstairs is a cozy alcove with a desk and large windows. The spacious downstairs living room is comfortably furnished and has a large fireplace. Breakfast is served in the formal dining room but is optional. Rates are $25 (single) to $35 (double) and reservations are required.

WOODLAND PARK

Seattle, WA
Pacific: 206 784-0539

Marit treats her guests as if she has friends visiting and, "If they're not important, who is?" Everything in Marit's home is an example of Scandinavian hospitality from the little note that reads, "My guests are worth a mint. Sweet dreams," to the gourmet breakfast served in the formal dining room. Marit's brick Tudor home is centrally located and is within walking distance of the zoo. The upstairs guest rooms are very cozy and comfortable. They are ideal for the business person on the go or for people who are looking for a homey environment. The bedrooms share a bathroom. One of the guest rooms (a single) offers a view of the Sound and the Olympic Mountains. Another is furnished with a queen-size bed, a desk, and has a sitting area. Rates are $25 (single) to $35 (double) and reservations are required.

GREEN LAKE

Seattle, WA
Pacific: 206 784-0539

Julia is the colorful and informal hostess of this Victorian guest house, which was built in 1890. She has been serving as a hostess for 18 years and is a retired English teacher. The upstairs master suite is the main facility for bed and breakfast. It includes a large bedroom, a small kitchenette, and a private bathroom. It also has a private elevator. A seating area by a large window offers a view of Green Lake and Woodland Park. The home is located just minutes from the interstate and downtown. Julia makes arrangements for breakfast based upon the needs of her guests. They can be served in the formal dining room or, if they choose, guests may prepare breakfast in their room. The rate for the master suite is $45 (double) and reservations are required.

LAKE CITY

Seattle, WA
Pacific: 206 784-0539

Astrid, your hostess, is a charming lady who loves to cook and makes every breakfast a special event. Homemade sourdough bread, sweet rolls, fresh fruit, and a delicious entree leave guests more than satisfied. Breakfast is served in either the formal dining room or a cozy breakfast nook that treats guests to lovely views of both Lake Washington and the Cascade Mountains. Astrid is also willing to provide other meals for her guests as long as they make prior arrangements with her. The home is conveniently located within five minutes of the interstate, ten minutes from the University District, and fifteen minutes from downtown. Two comfortable and cozy guest rooms are available. Astrid invites guests to relax in her large living room and enjoy a cup of their favorite hot beverage or sunbathe on the private deck that overlooks Lake Washington. Rates are $25 (single) to $35 (double) and reservations are required.

BALLARD

Seattle, WA
Pacific: 206 784-0539

These accommodations are perfectly suited for business people as well as other travellers. The upstairs guest rooms are homey, and a full breakfast is included. The roomy downstairs apartment is fully equipped. It has a private entrance, private bathroom, cable color television, private telephone, and a full kitchen that is well-stocked with food so that guests may prepare their own breakfast. Your hostess also offers the free use of her washer and dryer. The home's location provides quick and easy access to any point in town. It is just one-half block from bus service. Your hostess provides personal service. She has many maps and guides for her guests to use and is able to help them with information about the city. She also speaks German. Rates are $16 (single) to $35 (double) and reservations are required.

BALLARD

Seattle, WA
Pacific: 206 784-0539

On those rainy days for which Seattle has become famous, guests may choose to while away the hours in this large and private downstairs apartment – particularly if they are musical. In the spacious living room visitors are welcome to create their own concert on either the square grand piano or the pump organ. They may also enjoy a roaring blaze in the fireplace, reading a good book, or watching the color television. But on all those sunny days which Seattleites try to keep secret, guests will appreciate the fact that they are only minutes from Shilshole Bay, the Ballard Locks, the University District, and downtown Seattle. Virginia and Karre, owners of the home, are wonderful people and great conversationalists. Both served in the Peace Corps for two years and have travelled around the world. Rates are $35 (double) and reservations are required.

BALLARD

Seattle, WA
Pacific: 206 784-0539

Privacy is the key word when describing this downstairs apartment. It includes a private entrance for which guests are given their own key. A completely equipped kitchen is well-stocked with food for guests to prepare their own breakfast. The living room is quiet, carpeted, and has a fireplace. The bedroom is furnished with twin beds and closet space is plentiful. A covered patio and lovely yard provide guests with a place to relax. The home is located only a few blocks from the Woodland Park Zoo and Green Lake. It is ten minutes from downtown and fifteen minutes from the University District. Convenient bus service is available nearby. Rates are $30 (single) to $35 (double) and reservations are required.

BELLEVUE

Bellevue, WA
Pacific: 206 784-0539

This beautiful contemporary home sits on a wooded lot in a quiet subdivision. It is only five minutes from the interstate and twenty minutes from downtown Seattle. The owners, Rosemary and Ralph, are interesting people who love to share a glass of wine or sherry with their visitors while listening to classical music and perhaps discussing their favorite opera or the latest trend in art. Guests are welcome to enjoy the entire home. The spacious living room is dominated by a large stone fireplace and offers a partial view of Lake Washington. Sunbathers will appreciate the large deck on the upper level of the home. Breakfast is served on the oak table in the breakfast room and usually includes an entree, homemade baked goods, homemade jam, and fresh fruit. One guest room has a private full bathroom; the other has a private half bathroom. Rates are $30 to $35 for a double and reservations are required.

We are calling North Sound the portion of upper Puget Sound that comprises the San Juan Islands and Whidbey Island.

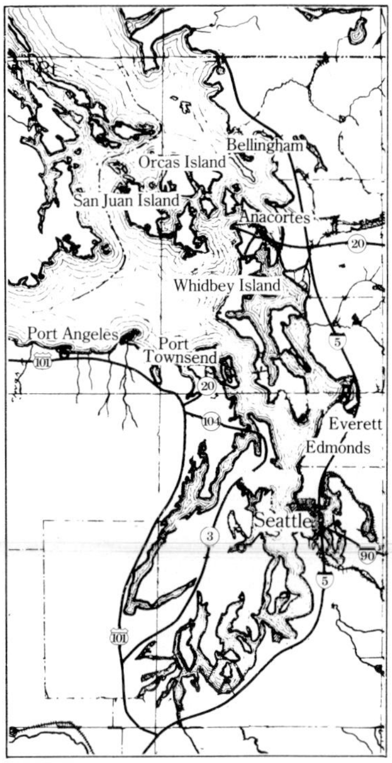

Your very own fantasy island awaits your arrival and is just a short ferry ride away. Beginning in Seattle, then north to Mukilteo and Anacortes, the Washington State Ferry System transports thousands of island travellers to an island paradise. During the busy tourist season lines of cars waiting to board the ferries will be long and slow-moving.

To reach Whidbey Island from the mainland, travellers may take the ferry from Mukilteo. From the Olympic Peninsula, visitors to Whidbey Island should board the ferry in Port Townsend. The island is also accessible by land over the Deception Pass Bridge via State Highway 20. Those of you travelling to the San Juan Islands will catch the ferries that leave from Anacortes.

Your ferry will carry you through narrow winding channels which weave past mostly rocky beaches that sparkle in the sun. Coves softly whisper their secrets to those who are listening as your ferry glides by.

Each island has been blessed with natural beauty and can be enjoyed for its rolling hills, rushing rivers, still and peaceful lakes, beaches, and coves. Sightseers from around the world begging a glimpse of island charm discover enchantment while touring in cars, on bicycles, and on foot.

Recreational opportunities abound. Boating and fishing lead the list. But there is ample opportunity for biking, hiking, clam digging, beachcombing, bird watching, and picnicking.

The San Juan Islands

Guidebooks and travel writers sometimes disagree on the exact number of islands that compose the chain, but all agree that there are at least 172 of them. Some are merely bumps of rock that seem to come and go with the tides. But most are lush with forests and are encircled by beaches.

Fishing is an angler's dream. King and silver salmon and various varieties of halibut and rockfish are abundant. The rocky beaches are alive with clams.

Orcas Island is the largest of the San Juans. The 5,000-acre Moran State Park has miles of hiking trails, a swimming beach, and trout fishing. One of the most spectacular views of the Northwest can be appreciated from atop Mt. Constitution.

The islands' largest town is Friday Harbor on San Juan Island. It is also the county seat of Island County. Two parks, San Juan National Historic Park and San Juan County Park, are located on the island.

Whidbey Island

Whidbey Island is the second largest island in the United States. Quaint villages pepper the landscape. Shopping and browsing adventures through art, craft, and specialty shops are plentiful.

The seaside communities of Langley and Coupeville are of particular interest to nostalgia hunters and history buffs. Both towns have maintained a turn-of-the-century character. Clinton, Freeland, and Greenbank offer travellers the peace and tranquillity they expect when visiting picturesque vacation spots but seldom find.

Beachcombers and nature lovers will frolic on the island's beaches, where they will discover an abundance of treasures. The tidelands host countless varieties of sea creatures. Clams, crabs, mussels, sea anemones, chitons, and limpets are just a few of the creatures that call the beach home.

Whidbey Island's six state parks offer an inviting list of activities including scuba diving, bicycling, beachcombing, boating, bird watching, hiking, and swimming. Joseph Whidbey, Fort Casey, Fort Ebey, South Whidbey, Ebey's Landing, and Deception Pass make up the island's state park system.

Deception Pass is one of the most, if not the most popular park in the state. It is thickly forested and offers hiking, beach walking, boating, and spectacular scenery.

POINTS OF INTEREST

Coupeville Whidbey Island
Deception Pass State Park Whidbey Island
Fort Casey State Park Whidbey Island
Friday Harbor San Juan Island
Holmes Harbor Whidbey Island (Freeland)
Moran State Park Orcas Island
Mt. Constitution Orcas Island
Oak Harbor Marina Whidbey Island
San Juan Island National Historic Park
Useless Bay Whidbey Island

PHONE NUMBERS

Washington State Ferries 1 800 542-0810

ADDRESSES

Central Whidbey Island Chamber of Commerce
P.O. Box 152
Coupeville, WA 98239

Greater Langley Chamber of Commerce
P.O. Box 403
Langley, WA 98260

North Whidbey Island Chamber of Commerce
5506 North Highway 20
Oak Harbor, WA 98277

Orcas Island Chamber of Commerce
P.O. Box 252
Eastsound, WA 98245

San Juan Island Chamber of Commerce
P.O. Box 302
Friday Harbor, WA 98250

SALLY'S BED & BREAKFAST MANOR

215 6th Street, Box 459
Langley, WA
98260 (Whidbey Island)
206 221-8709

Whidbey Island has long been a haven for artists and creative individuals. Sally DeFelice is one of them. She has created a lovely retreat in country elegance and has breathed spirit and charm into this 53-year-old farmhouse. Sally wanted to construct an environment in which people would get in touch with their feelings and leave her home rejuvenated. She has succeeded. The interiors give the home a feeling of peace and serenity. The furnishings are elegant yet comfortable. The guest rooms have private bathrooms. The living room is a wonderful place to curl up in front of a crackling fire, sip your favorite hot beverage, and ease back to ponder the meaning of life. An all-natural breakfast is served either in the solar sun room or in the formal dining room, where views of the Cascades and Saratoga Passage can be enjoyed. Rates are $50 (single) to $65 (double) and reservations are required.

WHIDBEY HOUSE

106 First Street
P.O. Box 156
Langley, WA
98260 (Whidbey Island)
206 221-7115

Everyone should awaken in this romantic and idyllic setting at least once. Dramatic views of Saratoga Passage, Camano Island, and the North Cascade Mountains are just a few of the reasons for visiting the Whidbey House. Hostess Priscilla Golas is the primary force behind the escapist environment found here. She is full of surprises and loves to pamper her guests. Following a peaceful night's sleep in this quiet spot by the water, guests will awaken to find their breakfast waiting in a picnic basket outside their door. While savoring their breakfast, guests will enjoy gorgeous views and perhaps even see a parade of whales. After their morning meal, guests may choose to take a walk along the beach, or escape for a day of boating, fishing, hiking, or shopping. Each of the home's three guest rooms has a private bathroom and rates are $55 for a double. Reservations are suggested.

THE ORCHARD

619 Third Street
Langley, WA
98260 (Whidbey Island)
206 221-7880

For those who are seeking a truly comfortable country setting, this old farmhouse surrounded by an orchard and hosted by Martha Murphy may be just the place. A quiet nature walk through a forest of fir and hemlock, picking fruits and nuts in the orchard, or reading your favorite book on the porch swing while the majestic Cascade Mountains wait patiently to catch your eye are just a few of the things that may make your stay a memorable one. Martha wants her guests to feel very much a part of her family. The two cozy upstairs bedrooms share a bathroom. The downstairs living room is warmed by an old wood stove. A big breakfast is served in the dining room. Martha welcomes children. Her home is open seven days a week during the summer. It is only available on weekends after Labor Day. Rates are $35 (single) to $50 (double) and reservations are suggested.

THE SARATOGA INN

4850 South Coles Road
Langley, WA
98260 (Whidbey Island)
206 221-7526

Twenty-five acres of forests and meadows surround this inn, which combines the comfort and convenience of a new structure with the warmth and tradition found in the best country houses. While guests lounge on the large sunny decks, they will marvel at the spectacular views of Saratoga Passage, Camano Head, and the Cascade Mountains. While they stroll the brick walkways and garden paths, guests will contemplate the beauty and splendor of gracious country living. For those guests who wish to tour antique shops, galleries, and stores, the quaint seaside village of Langley is only minutes away. Each of the guest rooms offers the finest in accommodations and has a private bathroom. The spacious living room has a large fireplace. Country antiques blend with fine Chippendale and Queen Anne furniture. Rates are $55 to $75 for a double and reservations are suggested.

KANGAROO HOUSE

North Beach Road
P.O. Box 334
Eastsound, WA
98245 (Orcas Island)
206 376-2175

This small country inn was named after the colorful pet of Captain Harold Ferris and his family, who lived in this stately home for more than 30 years. Ken and Polly Nisbet have chosen to retain the name. The home is located within a picturesque island setting that provides guests the opportunity to experience the quiet beauty of island life. Five restful bedrooms share one and one-half bathrooms. Guests can lounge on the deck or curl up in front of a crackling fire in the living room's fireplace. For guests who wish to quicken the pace, horseshoe pits are available for a friendly pitch. Bicyclists are welcome to keep their bikes in the bike rack under the deck. A home-cooked gourmet breakfast is served in the dining room. It may include locally grown fresh fruit and fresh-squeezed juice. Rates are $25 (single) to $45 (double) and reservations are suggested.

PILLARS BY THE SEA

1367 East Bayview Avenue
Freeland, WA
98249 (Whidbey Island)
206 221-7738

When guests visit this turn-of-the-century home, they immediately become an important part of Walker and Ellen Jordan's life story. "The house is the story of our life," Ellen says, "and we want people to share our little piece of America here." Both Walker and Ellen are warm, kind, caring, and friendly people who love to visit with their guests. The entire home has been elegantly decorated by Ellen, who is an interior decorator. There is a private entrance to the guest rooms from the deck. Both bedrooms share a bathroom. A warm and comfortable sitting room separates the guest rooms. A complete breakfast is served in the dining room, where guests will be able to enjoy both Ellen's homemade delicacies and spectacular views of historic Holmes Harbor and the Cascade Mountains. Rates are $40 (single) to $50 (double) and reservations are suggested.

CLIFF HOUSE

5440 South Grigware Road
Freeland, WA
98249 (Whidbey Island)
206 321-1566

Welcome to a world of luxury and elegance hidden away in a lush forest of madrone and tall fir. Peggy Moore's award-winning Cliff House, perched proudly on a bluff that overlooks Admiralty Inlet, is a soaring sophisticated marvel of architecture that becomes the exclusive home of only one guest couple at a time. Windows dominate the home. Upon awakening in the loft bedroom, guests are treated to incredible views of some of Mother Nature's finest work. Before coming downstairs for breakfast, guests may wish to ease their bodies into awareness while luxuriating in the soaking tub. Following breakfast visitors may descend the wooden staircase to the beach below and wander peacefully while listening to the waves lap the shore, enjoy a restful swing in the huge hammock, or take a soothing dip in the spa. Rates are $110 per night and reservations are suggested.

PALMER'S CHART HOUSE

P.O. Box 51
Deer Harbor, WA
98243 (Orcas Island)
206 376-4231

Palmer's Chart House is a unique and comfortable way to discover an island adventure. Overlooking Deer Harbor, the Chart House is a wonderful place to spend a day or a week. The setting is pastoral and the environment is warm and friendly. Guests will enjoy sitting on the private deck while viewing the yachts coming and going at the marina below. For those more adventurous spirits who wish to be a part of the seagoing parade, the Palmers' 33-foot yacht, Amante, is sometimes available for a sail with the Skipper. Don and Majean will join you at mealtime, or you may have your meal served in the privacy of your room. Both breakfast and dinner are included in the rates and everything is cooked in the Palmers' kitchen. Fresh fish is obtained from the local reef netters and fresh seasonal vegetables come from the Palmers' large vegetable garden. Rates are $30 per person per day and reservations are required.

WOODSONG

P.O. Box 32
Orcas, WA
98280 (Orcas Island)
206 376-2340

Carol and Alby Meyer have turned this remodeled schoolhouse, which is located only two miles from the ferry landing, into a wonderful country retreat. Nestled among towering evergreens, guests will have no trouble finding peace and tranquillity here. Before or after breakfast visitors will find enjoyment in a leisurely walk in the country. They may also wish to take advantage of the fine fishing found in nearby waters. Woodsong has been aptly named, as guests will find themselves serenaded by the many varieties of birds that nest on the grounds. It's a great place for bird watching, particularly in the spring and fall when the water birds are migrating. Fresh-cut flowers greet guests in their beautiful guest room. A breakfast of homemade goodies is served in the formal dining room. Rates are $26 (single) to $36 (double) and reservations are suggested.

PENN COVE INN

P.O. Box 628
Coupeville, WA
98239 (Whidbey Island)
206 678-6868

Dick and Joan approach each guest as an individual who has individual needs. "We want to be sensitive to our guests and their needs," Dick and Joan say. Whether it's reservations at one of the local restaurants or information to help bicyclists plan their trip, Dick and Joan are eager to provide assistance. There are three guest rooms in the cozy inn which share a bathroom. An elaborate breakfast of homemade muffins, bread, fresh fruit, a hot beverage, and juice is served on a linen tablecloth in the formal dining room. Guests are given their own private key to the house so that they may come and go as freely as they like. The Penn Cove Inn blends in with the quiet and peaceful atmosphere of the quaint village of Coupeville. Rates are $39 to $51 and reservations are suggested.

TUCKER HOUSE

260 B Street
Friday Harbor, WA
98250 (San Juan Island)
206 378-2783

Accommodations at the home of John and Evelyn Lackey include a cottage, a studio, and a downstairs bedroom in the main house. All guest rooms have a private bathroom and the cottage and studio have kitchen facilities. "We want people to feel at home, and we have tried to provide them with a place that's both comfortable and private," John and Evelyn say. The cottage is particularly suited for guests who are planning an extended visit. It is fully furnished, and has two private decks and a sleeping loft. The house is within easy walking distance of the ferry landing, airport, marina, and downtown shopping and restaurants. A complete breakfast is served in the recently completed and beautiful solarium. Rates are $35 to $60 for a double and reservations are suggested.

SAN JUAN HOTEL

50 Spring Street,
P.O. Box 776
Friday Harbor, WA
98250 (San Juan Island)
206 378-2070

Norm and Joan Schwinge are the owners of this charming hotel that was originally built in 1873. It still retains the spirit of those early days, but offers the comfort and convenience of today. Despite bearing the sign of a hotel, the San Juan has a home-like atmosphere in which guests will find themselves surrounded by friends. The ten guest rooms are furnished with antiques, many with brass or wicker beds. They share three large bathrooms. The handsome parlor, where breakfast is taken, is warmed by an antique parlor stove and affords guests views of the ever-changing harbor and neighboring islands. The parlor is a pleasant place to sip coffee, read the morning paper, and dream of an earlier day when life's pace seemed slower. The hotel is conveniently located one-half block from the ferry landing and is in the center of Friday Harbor. Rates are $26 (single) to $40 (double) and reservations are suggested.

COLLINS HOUSE

225 A Street
Friday Harbor, WA
98250 (San Juan Island)
206 378-5834

Leslie Stewart is the lovely and gracious hostess of this Victorian house that is within walking distance of both the ferry landing and downtown. Upon arriving, guests may find the house bathed in music, as Leslie loves to be surrounded by the sound of song. She wants people to enjoy the entire house and is sincerely interested in helping her guests with the planning of their trip. For those who leave their vehicles on the mainland, Leslie can make arrangements for them to rent mopeds or bicycles. Her home is completely furnished with antiques. Each of the three guest rooms has a private entrance. The parlor is a wonderful place to catch up on reading or to share quiet conversation. On sunny days Leslie encourages her visitors to take advantage of one of the three porches or the spacious back yard for an afternoon of sunbathing or lounging. Breakfast is served in the dining room and includes fresh ground coffee and locally grown fresh fruit. Rates are $40 to $45 for a double and reservations are suggested.

THE CHANNEL HOUSE

2902 Oakes Avenue
Anacortes, WA
98221
206 293-9382

This classic Victorian home is an ideal getaway and an unforgettable experience. Each room is furnished in antiques, has down comforters, and a peaceful ambiance that invites guests to forget their cares and woes. Besides being two very nice people, Sam and Kathy are in the business of spoiling guests. In the morning Kathy prepares a gourmet breakfast and serves it on fine family china. Fresh fruit grown on the grounds is available in season. Sam often invites guests to join him for a day of sailing aboard his 23-foot sloop. Visitors are also invited to take a dip in the hot tub. There are magnificent views of Puget Sound and the islands available from the house that sits on what Sam calls "the cleanest corner of the country." Rates are $33 (single) to $50 (double) and reservations are suggested.

HOME BY THE SEA

2388 East Sunlight
Beach Road
Clinton, WA
98236 (Whidbey Island)
206 221-2964

Sharon Fritts-Drew wants her guests to make themselves at "home by the sea." Sharon's waterfront home is located alongside the fjord-like Useless Bay and provides commanding views of the Olympic Mountains, Puget Sound, and Mt. Rainier. Both guest rooms are comfortably furnished and have private bathrooms. Sharon is casual and relaxed and hopes her guests will discover the value of quiet time. The beach has a tranquillizing and magical effect on guests who are invited to comb it for treasures or take a quiet nature walk among the geese, ducks, gulls, sandpipers, and herons that inhabit the natural bird sanctuary. Breakfast may include homemade yeast rolls, muffins, banana bread, cheese, and fresh ground coffee. Rates are $45 (single) to $55 (double) and reservations are required.

GUEST HOUSE

835 East Christenson Road
Greenbank, WA
98253 (Whidbey Island)
206 678-3115

Don and Mary Jane have created a unique bed and breakfast environment that will suit nearly every whim or need. Three private cottages, two country bedrooms in a 1920s farmhouse, and a magnificent log lodge are all located on 15 forested acres and await the traveller who is looking for something special. Each hide-away cottage is like a private home. All are cozy and furnished with antiques. The farmhouse bedrooms are warm, charming, and share a bathroom. The rustic lodge poses majestically above a wildlife pond and has all the amenities. The area is green and beautiful, and wildlife is abundant. Bald eagles soar overhead, deer roam throughout the property, and a croaking chorus of frogs sends guests' imaginations on a voyage to another era. Breakfast is optional in all accommodations and rates are lower if breakfast is not desired. Rates are $30 (single), $55 (cottage), $90 (lodge) and reservations are suggested.

Poulsbo, Bainbridge Island, Vashon Island, and Gig Harbor make up the area that we are calling South Sound.

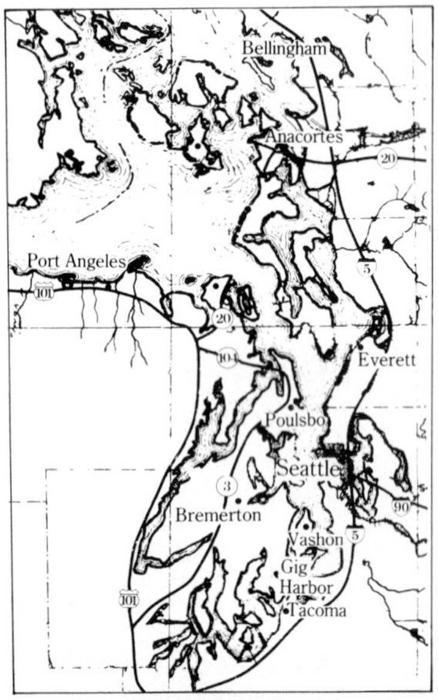

One of the ways that South Sound differs from North Sound is that many of the communities in the South Sound tend to serve as tiny suburbs for Seattle and Tacoma instead of travellers' tourist spots.

However, Poulsbo, Bainbridge Island, Vashon Island, and Gig Harbor do receive their share of visitors.

South Sound's two major islands are sparsely populated with tiny pockets of residential areas. Both Bainbridge and Vashon are easily accessible by ferry. The ride from the Seattle ferry dock to Winslow on Bainbridge Island is about 30 minutes. The island can also be reached from the north via Highway 305. Ferries will transport you to Vashon Island from both Fauntleroy (West Seattle) and Point Defiance in Tacoma.

South Sound is characterized by its charm and beauty. Rolling hills carpeted with dense forests and peaceful stretches of beaches make up the landscape. Bainbridge Island offers clear views of the Seattle skyline. Views of Mt. Rainier, Tacoma, and several Seattle suburbs are available from Vashon Island. Mt. Rainier peeks over the shoulder of Gig Harbor, and the Olympic Mountains stand guard over Poulsbo.

Hiking, biking, picnicking, shopping, museum-hopping, and auto-touring are the primary forms of recreation. The quiet roads that weave their way through both islands are ideal for bike excursions.

Poulsbo

Poulsbo is a small Scandinavian community that is sometimes referred to as "Little Norway." It is located a few miles north of Bainbridge Island and is accessible both by inland routes and via ferry. Visitors will particularly enjoy the "Norse" nature of many of the village's shops.

Bainbridge Island

This island suburb is an ideal place to escape Seattle's faster pace. It is only a few minutes ride by ferry from the city.

The ferry will dock at the island's only real town, Winslow, which has a population of about 2,400. A visit to the Bainbridge Arts and Crafts Gallery and a leisurely stroll along the marina are pleasant ways to spend a day. The town has several unique shops for browsing.

At the island's northeast corner is Fay Bainbridge State Park. It is a great place for a picnic, and the beach offers a grand view of Mt. Rainier. Fort Ward State Park is located at the south end and caters to the hiking enthusiast.

The Bainbridge Island Historic Museum at Strawberry Hill Park is a good way to learn about the history of the island. Suquamish Museum, which is just north of the island on the shores of Agate Passage, opens up the world of the Indians of Puget Sound through historical photographs and firsthand accounts of the original inhabitants.

Vashon Island

Vashon Island is centrally located via ferry between Seattle and Tacoma. A short ferry ride from West Seattle drops passengers off at the north end of the island. The south end is quickly arrived at via Point Defiance.

Its main attraction is the tranquillity it offers to auto-tourists and bicyclists who will find the quiet roads that meander through the thick woods ideal for peaceful and beautiful rides.

On the west side of Maury Island, visitors will find Dockton Park, which has picnic tables, playground equipment, and a boat moorage.

Gig Harbor

This small community began as a harbor for fishermen but now is more famous as a tourist village. There are several marinas, art and craft shops, and restaurants that make up the main business section of town.

For those of you who are seeking night life, the Tides Tavern, a shoreside establishment that also serves fine lunches, really comes alive when the stars come out, particularly on evenings when it features live music.

POINTS OF INTEREST

Bainbridge Island Historical Museum
Fay Bainbridge State Park
Bainbridge Island
Fort Ward State Park
Bainbridge Island
Suquamish Museum

PHONE NUMBERS

Washington State
Ferries 1 800 542-0810

ADDRESSES

Bainbridge Island Chamber of Commerce
166 Winslow Way East
Bainbridge Island, WA 98110

Gig Harbor Area Chamber of Commerce
3125 Judson Street
P.O. Box 1245
Gig Harbor, WA 98335

Poulsbo Chamber of Commerce
115 First Avenue
Poulsbo, WA 98370

Vashon Island Chamber of Commerce
P.O. Box 281
Vashon, WA 98070

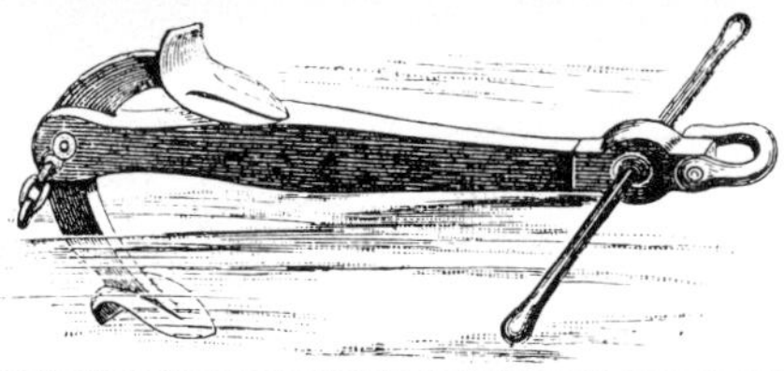

THE BOMBAY HOUSE

8490 N.E. Beck Road
Bainbridge Island, WA
98110
206 842-3926

In the words of one guest, "This house is a nice place to go back to and gets better with every visit." Visitors need not wonder why as they sit in the large living room, sip wine in front of a crackling fire, or enjoy their breakfast in the dining room while a chorus of songbirds serenades and soothes their souls. Bob and Georgene have done a marvelous job of providing a place for weary travellers that is truly a home away from home. The house is furnished in country antiques and is surrounded by masses of flowers that adorn the hillside. A gazebo and widow's walk add to the charm. Bob and Georgene are flexible and are fun to talk with. They can make arrangements for the use of canoes and bicycles. The house is also available for people who need a comfortable and private place for a colloquium. Rates are $39 to $75 for a double and reservations are suggested.

THE CAPTAIN'S HOUSE

234 Parfitt Way
Bainbridge Island, WA
98110
206 842-3557

Located in Winslow just four blocks from the ferry dock, The Captain's House is a turn-of-the-century home that overlooks Eagle Harbor. The cozy bedrooms are just what one might expect to find in a seafarer's home. They come complete with period furniture and fluffy comforters. Meg Hagemann is the gracious hostess who can arrange a special adventure for you aboard an 85-foot sailing vessel for a four-hour cruise and gourmet dinner or a six-hour picnic passage to Blake Island on a smaller vessel. She also provides the use of the Captain's skiff for those guests who wish to command their own ship. After an exciting sea adventure or a tour of the unique shops in Winslow, guests can return to the house and relax on the old porch swing while enjoying the view of the harbor and its sailing vessels. Rates are $30 to $45 for a double, reservations are suggested, and children are welcome.

PHOENIX HOUSE

10472 N.E. South Beach Drive
Bainbridge Island, WA
98110
206 842-7170

This guest cottage is truly a secluded getaway. For those who are looking for privacy and a chance to be alone for awhile, Phoenix House is ideal lodging. A private beach is only a short walk from the cottage. The beach offers spectacular views of Puget Sound, Mt. Rainier, and the Cascade Mountains. It is also a great place for beachcombing. Despite its seclusion, the house is located only 12 minutes from Winslow. The large guest room has a double bed, color television, and a comfortable sitting area. The private bathroom is adorned with wallpaper, has stained glass windows, and is highlighted by a brass claw-foot tub. Diane provides a rowboat and bicycles for her guests who may enjoy rowing in the Sound or biking along the waterfront. Rates are $36 (single) to $45 (double) and reservations are suggested.

THE SWAN INN

Route 5, Box 454
Vashon, WA
98070
206 463-3388

If it's a bit of jolly olde England that captures your fancy, then drive aboard the ferry to Vashon Island, and plan to spend a few days at this rustic country inn. The Swan Inn is a reconstruction of a 14th century English inn that is nestled in a farm setting and forest of tall firs reminiscent of rural England. Your hostess, Jeri Bain, has made several trips to England and has toured English inns. She has created a typically English ambiance in the inn complete with chimney pots, rustic iron hardware, and English antiques of the 17th and 18th centuries. After awaking to the rooster's crow and eating a farm-fresh breakfast, visitors will find that there is plenty to do on the island. Bicycling, hiking, horseback riding, boating, and fishing are just a few of the available activities. Rates are $35 (single) to $55 (double) and reservations are suggested.

THE SWALLOW'S NEST

Route 1, Box 221
Vashon, WA
98070
206 463-2646

These two guest cottages offer the discriminating traveller a country get-away that is only 25 minutes from Seattle. Perched on 20 acres of land, the farm-like accommodations overlook Puget Sound and provide a commanding view of Mt. Rainier. One of the cottages actually has nesting swallows residing outside of it. It also has a fully equipped kitchenette. Both cottages are tastefully decorated in a comfortable and warm manner with hanging plants and rocking chairs. Kathryn Keller keeps the cottages well supplied with tea, coffee, cocoa, books, and magazines. In the morning Kathryn greets guests with a gentle knock on their door signaling the arrival of breakfast, which may include homemade muffins, fresh berry jams, a hot beverage, and juice. Rates are $40 for stays longer than one night, and $50 for a one-night visit. Weekly rates are discounted and reservations are suggested.

THE OLDE GLENCOVE HOTEL

Route 4, Box 4616A
Gig Harbor, WA
98335
206 884-2835

Built as a resort hotel in 1896, The Olde Glencove Hotel has been a registered historic landmark since 1978. Owners Larry and Luciann Nadeau have been restoring it in an effort to portray a part of America as it once was. Guest accommodations include two private rooms, each with a sitting room and a private bathroom. Breakfast is prepared on an 87-year-old wood stove and is served either in the dining room by candlelight or brought to the guest rooms if weather permits. Larry is known locally for his horseshoe game and can usually be talked into a spirited and friendly contest. Nearby there are several state parks and the lovely and friendly town of Gig Harbor, as well as Tacoma and Bremerton, which are both only a thirty-minute drive away. The hotel is also available as a romantic setting for Victorian weddings. Rates are $40 per night and reservations are suggested.

NO CABBAGES

7712 Goodman Drive N.W.
Gig Harbor, WA
98335
206 858-7797

Picture the sun glistening off the blue waters of the harbor while Mt. Rainier looms picturesquely in the background. Your entire being is at peace with itself as you walk leisurely along the beach, occasionally stopping to inspect one of nature's treasures or to feel the sand between your toes. This world of peace and tranquillity is yours when you stay at the waterfront home of Jamee and Dal. Each of the guest rooms has a view of the harbor and shares a private entrance and a bathroom. Breakfast is served in a cozy dining room that overlooks East Gig Harbor, and guests can expect a delicious breakfast that will include homemade delicacies from Jamee's kitchen. Visitors are invited to take a moment to join Jamee and Dal in front of the stone fireplace in the living room for a bit of friendly conversation. Rates are $30 to $40 for a double and reservations are required.

HILLSIDE GARDENS

6915 Silver Springs
Drive N.W.
Gig Harbor, WA
98335
206 851-5007

Backpackers, bicyclists, skiers, and nature lovers of all kinds will particularly enjoy meeting Carol and Dick. Both are avid outdoors enthusiasts who love to share stories about their adventures and information about the area with visitors. Their home is located on a wooded lot in a quiet neighborhood. The beautifully landscaped yard is a great place to while away the hours while swinging in the hammock or sunbathing on the deck. Guests can be assured of a quiet night's sleep in the comfortable bedroom that comes with a private bathroom. Visitors are welcome to join Carol, Dick, and the family dogs, Lady and Little Bit, for a quiet evening in the living room. Breakfast is served in the formal dining room and includes fresh fruit that is grown on the property. Rates are $20 (single) to $30 (double) and reservations are required.

FJORD HOUSE

18290 Fjord Drive N.E.
Poulsbo, WA
98370
800 562-7455
(within Washington)
800 547-1463
(outside of Washington)

Michael and Wille Klinger look forward to welcoming their guests and showing off a beautiful corner of the world. Located just four blocks from the scenic Scandinavian village of Poulsbo, this waterfront home offers old-fashioned country hospitality and first-class accommodations. The home has one large bedroom with a private bathroom. Visitors can enjoy the gorgeous view of Liberty Bay and the Olympic Mountains from the privacy of their room. In the evening guests are invited to join Michael and Wille for conversation, tea, and cookies in the homey downstairs living room. A tasty full breakfast is served in the cozy dining room. Rates are $28 (single) to $40 (double) and reservations are suggested.

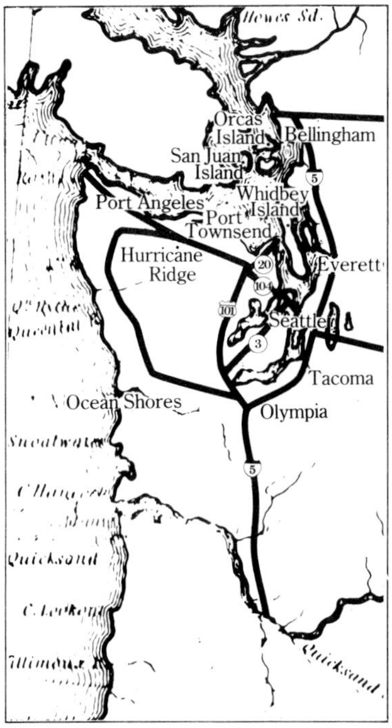

Ice-clad and snow-crested, the Olympic Mountains rise majestically 7,000 feet above the Pacific Ocean. These towers of strength overlook lush rain forests and some of the last wilderness beaches in the continental United States. It's as if Mother Nature took her finest ingredients, placed them in a tiny corner of the earth, and created the masterpiece we call the Olympic Peninsula.

Each year thousands of visitors come to this sparsely populated paradise to camp, hike, fish, and boat. They dig oysters and clams in season, savoring both what they find and the opportunity to enjoy this unspoiled land.

Washington's Pacific Coast boasts some of the finest deep-sea fishing in the United States. The intertidal zones surrounding the Peninsula are alive with a variety of shellfish. For those who want an opportunity to observe magnificent creatures of the sea, special whale-watching charters are available. There are also several excellent vantage points along the coast to view these living monoliths.

Colorful communities rich in history nestle between the mountains and the shoreline. Their residents are warm and friendly, and all who visit will leave with hearts full of fondness and heads full of memories.

Port Townsend

Port Townsend is a seacoast town that has been designated a National Historic District and boasts several excellent examples of Victorian architecture. It has an impressive community of painters, sculptors, weavers, potters, poets, and writers.

Its history is one of economic hopes never realized. In 1890 its prospects seemed limitless. Population had reached 7,000 and an array of Victorian houses and commercial buildings were erected; however, the proposed hook-up with the Union Pacific's transcontinental railroad never materialized and Port Townsend never became the hub of Puget Sound's commerce as it had once hoped.

Today the town retains the look and feel of a small Victorian seaport. Its residential community, perched on a bluff overlooking the small business district, has retained its turn-of-the-century look. Many of the commercial structures have been restored to reflect that bygone era.

The town has several full-service marinas and launching ramps. Salmon fishing is excellent and there are good clam, crab, and oyster beaches.

There are several festivals that visitors may enjoy. In mid-May the Rhododendron Festival is celebrated with a week of parades, carnivals, flower shows, and special events. The Centrum Foundation presents its Celebration of American Arts each summer. And in early September the Wooden Boat Festival and Symposium is held.

Port Angeles

Port Angeles is the gateway to the Olympic Mountains. A short drive brings visitors to Hurricane Ridge in the Olympic National Park. Hurricane Ridge offers spectacular views of the Olympic Mountains and the Strait of Juan de Fuca. In winter it also offers the snowshoer and cross-country skier relatively dry and moderately deep snow, compliments of its altitude and eastern exposure.

Salmon and halibut fishermen make Port Angeles their base, and freshwater fishermen will want to explore the nearby Elwha River for steelhead and Lake Crescent for trout. Hikers will also want to discover these areas, both of which serve as trailheads to the high country.

Ocean Shores

This coastal resort city beckons visitors to frolic on its sandy Pacific beaches, dig for clams, or jump aboard one of the charters in its small fleet to enjoy a day of deep-sea fishing.

Ocean City State Park is only a short drive from Ocean Shores and spreads out across rolling dunes. The entire family will enjoy picnicking, ocean swimming, and fishing.

A virus seriously affected the state's razor clam population in 1983. The Fish and Game Department restricted harvesting to protect the clam population. Visitors interested in digging for this popular shellfish should check with local authorities on the status of these restrictions.

POINTS OF INTEREST

Clallum County Museum Port Angeles
Hood Canal Floating Bridge links the Kitsap and Olympic Peninsulas
Hurricane Ridge eighteen miles south of Port Angeles
Manis Mastodon Site Sequim
Neuharth Winery Sequim
Of Sea & Shore Museum Port Gamble
Pope & Talbot Historical Museum Port Gamble
Port Townsend Museum
Sequim-Dungeness Museum Sequim

PHONE NUMBERS

Highway Patrol	206 478-4646
Olympic National Park	206 452-4501
Parks and Recreation	206 753-2027
Victoria Ferry	206 457-4491
Washington State Ferries	206 464-6400 or 1-800-542-0810

ADDRESSES

Olympic National Park
600 East Park Avenue
Port Angeles, WA 98362

Olympic Peninsula Travel Association
c/o Washington State Ferries
Seattle Ferry Terminal, Pier 52
Seattle, WA 98104

Port Townsend Chamber of Commerce
2437 Sims Way
Port Townsend, WA 98368

STARRETT HOUSE INN

744 Clay Street
Port Townsend, WA
98368
206 385-5619

Standing tall and reaching toward the sky, this marvel of Victorian architecture is grand and elegant. Its nine rooms are each distinguished. Richard and Susan Thompson want their guests to leave feeling as if they've been treated to the best sleep they've had in weeks and that they are part of the growing Starrett House family. The rates include tea or coffee delivered to the guest's room on a silver service and a champagne breakfast served in the main floor dining room. The restaurant is open Friday, Saturday, and Sunday nights for a pleasurable and unique dining experience. It features a large selection of wines from the Starrett's wine cellar. Susan is the chef whose forte is pastry. Rates are $40 (single) to $80 (double) and reservations are suggested.

QUIMPER INN

1306 Franklin
Port Townsend, WA
98368
206 385-1086

Walk into the Quimper Inn and enter a world that is like no other. Every wall, nook, and cranny has been embellished in an artist's palette of panache. This 1880 Georgian house is truly a feast for the eyes. The artist is Mariii. She has taken part in the creation of a comfortable guest house that is also a gallery. Paul joins Mariii in this creative environment and both are readily available to provide personal attention to each of their guests. Each guest room is special and has its own celebrated view. Both private and shared bathrooms are available. After awaking from a good night's sleep and eating a delicious breakfast, guests may choose to stroll along the sandy beaches, tour historic Port Townsend, or bike a country lane. In the evening guests are welcome to enjoy the common room which features a growing art library and gallery or take a soothing dip in the hot tub. Rates are $45 to $75 for a double and reservations are suggested.

JAMES HOUSE

1238 Washington Street
Port Townsend, WA
98368
206 385-1238

The James House was the first bed and breakfast guest house in the Northwest and continues the tradition of warmth and hospitality today. Innkeepers Deborah and Rod LaMontagne stress rest and solitude. Silence is the password, but warmth is the key. According to Deborah, it's a great place to escape to and avoid stress. The house, built by Francis James in 1891, is a grand Victorian mansion that has spacious rooms furnished in period antiques, some original to the house. Garden suites and a bridal suite are available. The bridal suite was originally the master bedroom and has a fireplace, original parquet floor, claw-foot tub, and a private balcony off the bay-windowed sitting room. The main floor of the house invites guests to relax and converse comfortably in either of two parlors, each with a fireplace, or the dining room. Breakfast is served in the kitchen. Rates are $38 (single) to $80 (double) and reservations are suggested.

LIZZIE'S

731 Pierce
Port Townsend, WA
98368
206 385-4168 or 385-9826

"Lizzie's and Port Townsend deserve a delicacy of perception," Thelma says. And she is so right. This Victorian residence, originally constructed in 1897, is so completely embellished that a careful and observant pair of eyes will be delightfully pampered. Lizzie's guests have an opportunity to luxuriate in surroundings which include handworked antiques and Belgian and Oriental rugs. Seven lovely guest rooms provide visitors with an elegance unmatched by modern accommodations yet bathed in the warmth and hospitality of a private residence. The entire house is to be used and enjoyed. Guests are encouraged to relax in the main floor parlor or living room and enjoy the crackling fire. Rates are $49 to $79 for a double and reservations are suggested.

HASTINGS HOUSE INN

313 Walker
Port Townsend, WA
98368
206 385-3553

The Hastings House Inn offers guests a rare opportunity to step back in time and experience a Victorian home as it was in 1889. Perched upon a bluff high above town, the home commands a magnificent view of both Admiralty Bay and the Cascade Mountains. Bruce and Grace encourage a quiet and peaceful atmosphere where guests can ease back, take a deep breath, and relax. The parlor, which looks out on the bay, is adorned with an old pot belly stove and has a library that includes many old magazines which date back as far as the late 1800s. Each room offers its own special unique surprise and is furnished with finely crafted antiques. The ivory tower adjacent to the Ivory Room has to be seen to be believed. It is a great place to sit for hours and contemplate your dreams or just while away the afternoon. Both private and shared bathrooms are available. Rates are $35 (single) to $75 (double) and reservations are suggested.

OCEAN SHORES

Ocean Shores, WA
BABS: 206 733-8642

The seashore location of this home makes it unique among Washington bed and breakfast homes. The guest room is a downstairs bedroom with a private bath and is available from June until the middle of September. Breakfast is included in the rates, and additional meals are available by prior arrangement. Doris and Thomas speak French and Spanish and enjoy crafts, swimming, bicycling, and photography. Guests can take leisurely walks among the sand dunes or just relax on the beach. For those who wish to quicken the pace, swimming and surfing are available. And for those who are seeking an adventure, sport salmon fishing is very popular here. Children are welcome and sleeping "pads" for as many as three children are available. Rates are $22 (single) to $28 (double) and reservations are required two weeks in advance. Description Provided By Agency.

THE TUDOR INN

1108 South Oak
Port Angeles, WA
98362
206 452-3138

Located within minutes of the Victoria, B.C. ferry and only eighteen miles from the Olympics' Hurricane Ridge, this turn-of-the-century English Tudor inn has been tastefully restored to capture the charm and atmosphere of an earlier era. Jane and Jerry Glass are dedicated to making their guests comfortable. Five guest rooms, each with a view of either the Olympic Mountains or the Strait of Juan de Fuca, share two spacious bathrooms. In the summer there is great salmon fishing nearby and guests can hike, climb, and enjoy the beauty and splendor of the Olympic Mountains. In the winter the inn offers a weekend cross-country ski package to Hurricane Ridge that will appeal to the novice as well as the advanced skier. Rates are $30 (single) to $45 (double) and reservations are suggested. Special rates are available in the winter.

McLEROY HOUSE

139 West 14th
Port Angeles, WA
98362
206 457-3424

Edith and Charles McLeroy like to describe themselves as just an elderly couple with a house on the side of the road waiting for guests to arrive. The McLeroys are proud that they take time to talk to their guests and that guests frequently become friends. Both Edith and Charles are eager to help visitors enjoy their trip to the area. The home is within walking distance of Olympic Park headquarters and only 18 miles from Hurricane Ridge. Both hiking and fishing are available nearby as well as cross-country skiing in the winter. Guest rooms have both private and shared bathrooms. One of the bedrooms has a view of the strait. Breakfast may include Edith's specialty of sourdough biscuits or guests may be treated to Charles' specialty of pancakes. There is a fireplace and television in the living room which guests are welcome to enjoy. Rates are $20 (single) to $28 (double) and reservations are suggested.

Like an arrow flying straight and true, Interstate 5 leads thousands of visitors north from Seattle, through Everett and Bellingham, to Vancouver, B.C. Its spurs direct people to the North Cascades and the North Sound. This chapter covers those mainland areas just east and west of the interstate and includes the city of Bellingham.

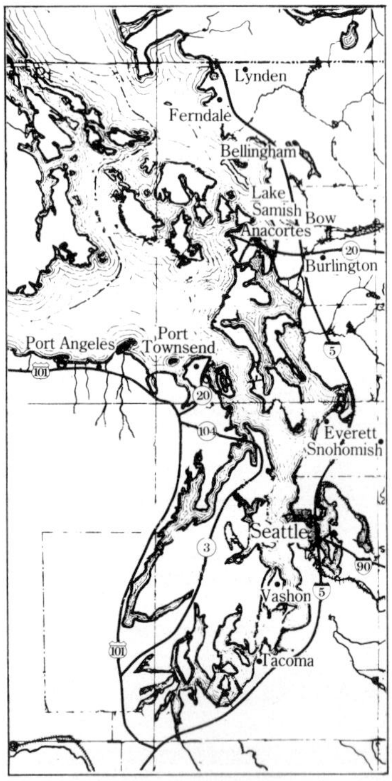

Everett and Bellingham are the two major cities in Northwest Washington.

Everett has long been a lumber port and mill town. It is also the home of the Boeing assembly plant for 747s, which is located at Paine Field. Only a short drive east of Everett is the historic community of Snohomish, which has several excellent examples of Victorian architecture and dozens of antique shops.

Bellingham is located on the northeast shore of Bellingham Bay. It is 54 miles south of Vancouver and 86 miles north of Seattle. The Port of Bellingham dominates commercial activity within the city.

Northwest Washington boasts the largest dairy county in the United States. In the spring the landscape presents a cornucopia of color when irises, daffodils, and tulips blossom.

As is true in so much of the Evergreen State, recreational opportunities are everywhere.

Lakes, rivers, streams, and the bay are home to bass, trout, and salmon. If you don't feel like fishing in the waters of Northwest Washington, perhaps you'd like to raft down them. The Skagit, Stillaguamish, and the Skykomish will shoot you through narrow whitewater canyons and float you along river deltas.

The North Cascade Range is a short, scenic drive from the interstate via Highway 20. Once there hikers and skiers alike will find all the necessary ingredients to make the trip worthwhile. North of Bellingham, Highway 542 leads hikers and skiers to Mt. Baker. From November to May the area offers great downhill skiing.

For museum fanciers the Whatcom Museum of History and Art in Bellingham is a must. Northwest painters are well-represented and displays that tell the story of local logging are dynamic. The Bellingham Maritime Heritage Center is open to visitors who wish to learn more about the Northwest's maritime industries.

There are several parks along Interstate 5 worth investigating. Wenberg State Park is 18 miles north of Everett via exit 206. It sits alongside Lake Goodwin and offers fishing, boating, and swimming. The Hovander County Park near Ferndale provides visitors with a chance to see a typical Northwest farm environment. There are also some very good views of Mt. Baker from the grounds.

POINTS OF INTEREST

Boeing Assembly Plant Everett
Hovander County Park Ferndale
Lake Padden Bellingham
Mt. Baker Highway 542
Peace Arch State Park Canadian border, exit 276
Port of Bellingham
Snohomish
Wenberg State Park Lake Goodwin, exit 206
Whatcom Museum of History and Art Bellingham

ADDRESSES

Everett Chamber of Commerce
P.O. Box 1086
Everett, WA 98206

Snohomish Chamber of Commerce
P.O. Box 135
Snohomish, WA 98290

Bellingham-Whatcom Visitors and Convention Bureau
P.O. Box 340
Bellingham, WA 98227

LAKE SAMISH

Bellingham, WA
BABS: 206 733-8642

If water sports and beautiful scenery appeal to you, then this home may be just right. Located just a few miles south of the city of Bellingham, this waterfront home offers accommodations that overlook lovely Lake Samish. Swimming, fishing, boating, and water-skiing are just some of the activities waiting a few feet from your guest room. Both bedrooms share a bathroom and have a view of the lake and Lookout Mountain. Guests are also invited to use the family room and the recreation room. Both rooms have a fireplace. A piano waits patiently for your musical enjoyment in the recreation room. A continental breakfast, which sometimes features Dolores's homemade blueberry muffins, is served in the upstairs dining room. Rates are $22 (single) to $28 (double) and reservations are required.

BELLINGHAM

Bellingham, WA
BABS: 206 733-8642

This old farmhouse is furnished throughout with antiques and sits on eight acres of forest and pasture. Donald is retired from the post office and enjoys organic gardening, stamp collecting, people, and conversation. For those who wish a full breakfast, Mary Jane specializes in buttermilk hot cakes. Additional meals featuring home-grown food are available by prior arrangement. Accommodations include two rooms with double beds. The rooms share a bathroom. Both rooms have recently been redecorated. The home is conveniently located near shopping, a bus line, the interstate, and the airport. Rates are $18.50 (single) to $22.50 (double) and reservations are required. Description Provided By Agency.

WARNER HOUSE

611 North Garden Street
Bellingham, WA
98225
206 671-0995
or 676-9884

Your hostess, Jean, is an interior designer who has her own gallery. She is warm and friendly and wants to share her interests in art and architecture with guests. Her home is particularly suited for visitors to Western Washington State University. Located right across the street from the university, the home provides easy access to the people and events on the campus. Western's Outdoor Museum, which displays several world-class sculptures, and several other art galleries are within a few minutes of the home. The guest rooms share a bathroom. One of the upstairs bedrooms overlooks Bellingham Bay and the working harbor. Its large windows offer a panoramic view. Conveniences in the room include a color television, desk, and telephone. Jean encourages her guests to relax on the downstairs sun deck. Rates are $30 (single) to $40 (double) and reservations are suggested.

BURLINGTON

Burlington, WA
BABS: 206 733-8642

Located only one-fourth of a mile from the interstate, this luxurious home overlooks the Skagit Valley and the approach to the North Cascades Highway. Helen, a retired school teacher, and Tilman, a carpenter, are the owners of this beautiful home. Both guest rooms have private bathrooms. One of the guest rooms is furnished with a queen-size bed, the other with a double bed. Hiking, cascading rivers, scenic lakes, Puget Sound, and the Cascade Mountains are nearby. A continental breakfast is included in the rates, which are $15 (single) to $20 (double). Reservations are required. Description Provided By Agency.

CHUCKANUT BED & BREAKFAST

312 Blanchard Road
Bow, WA
98232
206 766-6940

Breakfast with Don and Carol sometimes goes on for hours because they both enjoy people so much. They particularly love to talk about travelling. Both are eager to help their guests with travel plans and are able to provide many recommendations for things to do in the area. Their home is located within easy driving distance of Deception Pass and the San Juan Islands' ferry dock. The accommodations are apartment-like and include a kitchenette and a private bathroom. Breakfast is served in the upstairs living room that is furnished comfortably and has an old wood stove. If guests tire of hiking along the many trails located nearby on Chuckanut and Blanchard Mountains or grow weary of the great bicycling that's available to them, they may lounge on the home's roomy deck that overlooks Samish Bay and the San Juan Islands. Rates are $28 for a double and reservations are suggested.

SAMISH ISLAND

Bow, WA
BABS: 206 733-8642

Children are welcome to this waterfront home on Padilla Bay. Fred and Susan have three young daughters and can make arrangements for baby-sitting. The accommodations include a cozy bedroom with a double bed. During the summer months a beach house that will accommodate guests with sleeping bags is available. It has a sink and a fireplace. Fred and Susan invite guests to use their canoe. Guests are also welcome to enjoy the beach, which is a great place to relax or to dig clams. Rates are $15 (single) to $18 (double) and reservations are required. Description Provided By Agency.

COUNTRYMAN'S

119 Cedar
Snohomish, WA
98290
206 568-9622

If you've ever wanted to spend a night or two in an art gallery, here's your chance. The entire home, including the upstairs guest rooms, is an art museum. Pieces include everything from limited edition prints to locally produced works. The Victorian-style cedar home is listed on the National Historic Register and was built in 1896. As well as offering guests an opportunity to stay in a historically significant home that is also an art gallery, Larry and Sandy give guests an added bonus. Included in the rates is a tour of the area's historic homes, during which Larry and Sandy provide information about each home. Guests are invited to choose their breakfast menu. Children are welcome. Sometimes one of Larry and Sandy's children is available for baby-sitting. Rates are $40 to $45 for a double and reservations are suggested.

FERNDALE

Ferndale, WA
BABS: 206 733-8642

Alice and Paul have had visitors from around the world. Surrounded by 500 acres of scenic pastures, this working dairy farm offers a "down-home" atmosphere and an opportunity for guests to see a dairy farm in operation. Breakfast is served in the farmhouse kitchen, which is adorned with family antiques. But if you're an early riser and get up at milking time, you can expect to pour your own coffee. By prior arrangement, other family-style meals may be provided. One of the guest rooms has a private bathroom. As well as operating the dairy farm, Alice and Paul have done some travelling to other countries. Rates are $15 (single) to $18 (double) and reservations are required. Description Provided By Agency.

LYNDEN

Lynden, WA
BABS: 206 733-8642

Snowcapped Mt. Baker provides the backdrop for this cozy two-bedroom guest cottage. It is completely self-contained with a kitchen, living room, and bathroom. Mildred and Frank are retired dairy farmers. They still own one hundred acres of land and have a few cows and calves around to keep them busy. The guest cottage and the main house are surrounded by manicured lawns and lovely flowers. A continental breakfast is included in the rates, but a full breakfast and other meals can be made available by prior arrangement. The guest house is accessible to anyone who may be confined to a wheelchair. Rates are $18 (single) to $20 (double) and reservations are required. Description Provided By Agency.

CASCADE  MOUNTAINS

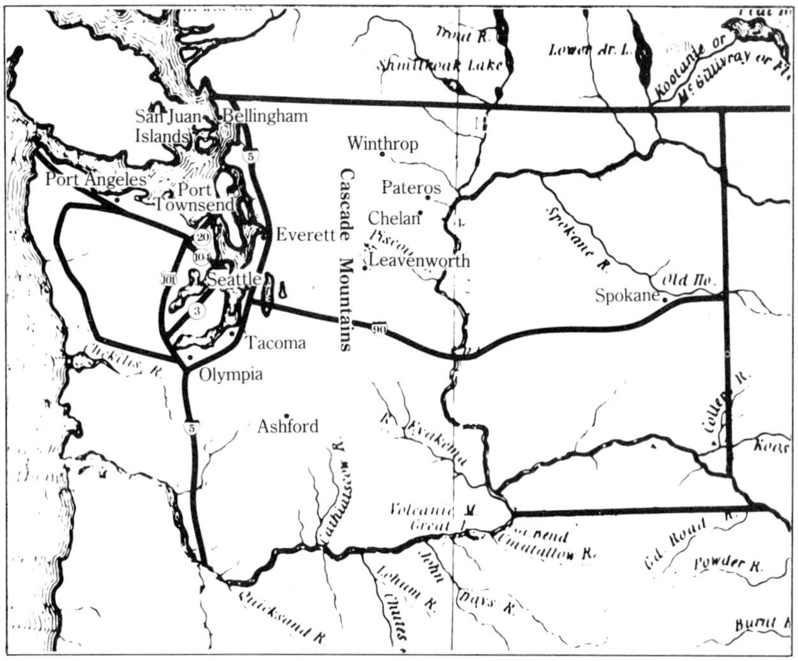

From the rolling foothills and Alpine meadows bursting with color, to the soaring steep-walled peak and awesome beauty of Mt. Rainier, the Cascade Mountains are a tribute to the power and glory of nature. Visitors from around the world come to revel in these mountains of rock and ice.

Hikers can choose from hundreds of trails. Some are gentle and kind, just right for a leisurely day hike; others are steep and tortuous, challenging to the most skilled. Campers can pitch their tents in base camps surrounded by like-minded enthusiasts, or they can head into the wilderness to their own private glacial lake or raging river.

Mountaineers from novice to Everest-bound can find a climb that will satisfy their craving for beauty and will challenge their hearts, minds, and bodies.

In winter deep snows attract thousands to the area. Downhill and cross-country skiers delight in the powder atop a packed base. Snowshoers find themselves in a winter paradise that is hard to match.

Most of the Cascades are composed of federal park land, and access to the mountains has been made relatively easy. Four major highways lead to the passes. The North Cascades Highway, U.S. 2, Interstate 90, and U.S. 12 are direct routes into the mountains.

Mt. Rainier National Park is the most popular and heavily used area in the Cascades. When the peak is not shrouded in clouds, roads leading to the park are jammed with mountain-goers eager to heap praise upon the giant.

As well as being one of the most beautiful and spectacular sights in the United States, this picture-postcard peak is famous for its records. It has recorded the world's greatest snowfall. It has 26 glaciers – the most of any single mountain in the United States, excluding Alaska. And it is the highest volcanic summit in the contiguous United States.

But Mt. Rainier National Park is not the only outlet for recreation among these peaks. Ski areas, campgrounds, and resorts make recreation the area's most popular pastime.

The Cascades are not only a formidable barrier separating east from west, but they are the reason for the differences in vegetation and climate as well.

The wet west side of the range is graced with deep verdant valleys and lush forests of fir and hemlock. The east side is sunny and dry with expanses of meadow and columns of pine.

Dozens of tiny communities nestle snugly against the mountains. They survive the harshest of Washington's weather. Each is unique and each offers its own brand of adventure.

Ashford

The tiny community of Ashford is located just six miles from the Nisqually entrance of Mt. Rainier National Park. This entrance leads to Longmire (park headquarters), Paradise (the park's best-known visitor center), and several major campgrounds.

The surrounding area is ideal for hikers, mountaineers, and sightseers. Visitors may enjoy jumping aboard the Mt. Rainier Scenic Railroad, which is in nearby Elbe. There is ample opportunity for shoppers to browse through the many craft and novelty shops in the area.

Chelan

Rolling camel-back hills surround this lively resort community that is at the southeast corner of Lake Chelan. Boating dominates the spirit of the community. There is a large park at the edge of town and an 18 hole golf course for putters and duffers. Lake Chelan State Park is nine miles west of Chelan.

Pateros

Pateros is a lovely community that is located about 20 miles from Lake Chelan. In the summer boating, water-skiing, and fishing are excellent. In the winter the Methow Valley offers some of the finest cross-country skiing in the state. There are also many snowmobile trails both in the valley and in Pateros.

Leavenworth

In 1960 Leavenworth's tumble from a thriving railroad and logging town to its near demise was almost complete. But then something beautiful happened. Members of the community were determined to halt the town's nose dive and they did.

Project L.I.F.E. (Leavenworth Improvement For Everyone) was born. Out of it came the rebirth of a town in the nature of the Swiss Alpine look.

Leavenworth plays host each year to about 800,000 visitors who come from every corner of the world to see this Bavarian village.

As well as the many shops rich in European goods, there is recreation galore. White water rafting on the Wenatchee River, lakes and rivers rich in trout and other game fish, hiking, climbing, bicycling, jogging, horseback riding, cross-country skiing, and snowmobiling are all available for those who enjoy the great outdoors.

The town is particularly busy on festival weekends. The Mai Fest is held in May; Autumn Leaf Festival in September and October; and the Christmas Lighting Festival in December.

Winthrop

Bring along your Stetson and cowboy boots when you visit the old west town of Winthrop. Located in the upper Methow Valley, it is surrounded almost completely by national forest or state game range.

It boasts of being an outdoor paradise featuring fishing, hunting, skiing, hiking, swimming, and snowmobiling.

POINTS OF INTEREST

Lake Chelan National Recreation Area
Leavenworth
Mt. Rainier National Park
North Cascades Highway
White Pass Ski Area
Winthrop

ADDRESSES

Chelan Chamber of Commerce
P.O. Box 216
Chelan, WA 98816

Leavenworth Chamber of Commerce
226 8th Street
Leavenworth, WA 98826

Mt. Rainier National Park
Longmire, WA 98397

Pateros Chamber of Commerce
General Delivery
Pateros, WA 98846

Winthrop Chamber of Commerce
P.O. Box 402
Winthrop, WA 98862

HAUS ROHRBACH PENSION

12882 Ranger Road
Leavenworth, WA
98826
509 548-7024

Nestled at the base of Tumwater Mountain, Haus Rohrbach is a true European-style country inn where a smorgasbord of activities awaits the inn's guests. For those who are seeking adventure, nearby there is white-water rafting, hiking, fishing, and cross-country skiing. For those who prefer a slightly slower pace, the inn is just minutes from the Bavarian village of Leavenworth with its many shops and restaurants. And for those who really want to slow down the pace, the inn's swimming pool and hot tub beckon the guests to luxuriate in their warm crystal-clear waters year round. The inn's proprietors, Greg, Sharon, Bob, and Kathryn, try to encourage a home atmosphere in the inn, which has 13 guest rooms as well as a chalet. Children are welcome. Rates are $42 to $48 for a double and $65 for the chalet. Reservations are suggested.

EDEL HAUS

320 9th Street
Leavenworth, WA
98826
509 548-4412

This lovely home is located just one block from the specialty shops and restaurants of Leavenworth. Travellers from around the world enjoy the homey atmosphere and personal attention provided by Mark and Betsy Montgomery. Guests may relax in the hot tub or they may browse the nearby shops. Mark and Betsy can also arrange faster-paced adventures for those who dare. In the summer they can arrange bike tours, river rafting, horseback riding, and hay rides. Or they can suggest good swimming, hiking, and climbing areas. And in the winter a Scottish Lakes Nordic ski package offers guests a wilderness skiing experience that is a dream come true for cross-country skiing enthusiasts. Rates are $30.50 (single) to $50 (double) and there are special group packages available. Reservations are suggested.

BROWN'S FARM

11150 Highway 209
Leavenworth, WA
98826
509 548-7863

Steve and Wendi Brown would like to welcome you to a dream come true. It took twelve years to achieve, but now they have their big country house made out of hand-hewn logs. The guest rooms, a big farm kitchen, and an informal living room with a rock fireplace (in front of which may lie Brown Dog and Barney, family pets who are as friendly and warm as Steve and Wendi) are on the main floor. The farmhouse sits on three acres and is nestled on the side of a mountain. And don't bother to bring an alarm clock. The first cock-a-doodle-doo echoes from the hen house at the crack of dawn, just in time for you to roll over and go back to sleep. There are mountain trails to hike, eggs to gather, and rabbits to hug. Children are welcome. Breakfast is all you can eat and is farm fresh. Rates are $40 to $45 for a double and reservations are suggested.

McCLAIN'S BED AND BREAKFAST

1226 Front Street
Leavenworth, WA
98826
509 548-7755

This unique bed and breakfast retreat is just two blocks from Leavenworth village and offers a great view of the Cascade Mountains. Dora and Dale McClain have created an environment that is hard to resist. Whether you choose to luxuriate in the hot tub or shoot a game of pool in the spacious recreation room, you are sure to enjoy your stay at McClain's. The two guest rooms each have a private bathroom. One of the guest facilities is an apartment-size suite complete with kitchen, king-size waterbed, cable television, a breakfast nook, and a private deck. There are two ten-speed bicycles that are available for guests. Visitors are also welcome to use the laundry room. Breakfast is a real treat. Dora loves to feed people and is really pleased when they ask for seconds. Rates are $49 to $59 for a double and reservations are suggested.

HOLZSCHNITZER HAUS

3 Wilson Street
Leavenworth, WA
98826
509 548-4576

Perched on the banks of the Wenatchee River, Holzschnitzer Haus and its owners, Margot and Gunther Geyer, surround their guests with a typical European atmosphere. When you arrive, Margot and Gunther will greet you with a friendly cup of coffee or tea, and when you leave, a little souvenir from the Gunthers will be tucked away in your baggage. A totally German breakfast that may include German rye bread and German salami is served in the large dining room. There are two guest bedrooms that are both furnished with queen-size beds. Although peace and quiet are the main ingredients at Holzschnitzer Haus, Margot and Gunther can arrange for you to take an airplane sightseeing tour of the area. Rates are $42 for a double and reservations are required.

LAKE PATEROS BED & BREAKFAST

206 West Warren
Pateros, WA
98846
509 923-2626

When you enter this colonial-style house, you are sure to feel as if you have just stepped into a page right out of "Better Homes and Gardens." To say that Charlene and Bob Knoop have created a dream home would be an understatement. Crisp navy blues and springtime greens create a refreshing ambiance for the weary traveller, while antiques blend in perfect harmony with other, more contemporary, furnishings for a comfortable setting. Charlene likes to pamper her guests, and there is evidence of that throughout the home. From the down pillows and homemade quilts in the bedrooms to the full American-style breakfast that is served in the Knoop's dining room, guests are treated regally. Visitors will discover an abundance of recreational opportunities nearby. Children are welcome. Rates are $35 to $40 for a double and reservations are suggested.

THE ASHFORD MANSION

Box G
Ashford, WA
98304
206 569-2739

Built in 1903, this Georgian-style house may be just the place for you to stay when you visit Mt. Rainier National Park. The twelve-room mansion is located just six miles from the Nisqually park entrance. The home has two guest rooms that share a bathroom. Walt and Jan Green invite their guests to enjoy both the sitting room and the parlor. In the parlor guests may want to relax in front of the fireplace or play a melody on the grand piano. Before embarking on a day of hiking, mountain climbing, sightseeing, or a leisurely browse through the many craft and novelty shops in the area, guests are treated to a breakfast that includes a variety of breads and muffins, fresh fruit and berries in season, blackberry jam, and an entree. Rates range from $28 (single) to $38 (double) and reservations are suggested. Description Provided By Host.

DAMMANN BED AND BREAKFAST

716 Highway 20 South
Winthrop, WA
98862
509 996-2484

Operating a bed and breakfast home is as natural to Jean Dammann as breathing is to most of us. Her folks were in the hotel business for 27 years, so Jean has been around people all her life. That's the way she wants to keep it. Her home is located alongside the Methow River and is less than one mile from downtown Winthrop. Guests have a private entrance to their room and are invited to lounge on the deck and patio that overlook the river. The home is perfect for outdoorsmen. Nearby fishing, hunting, snowmobiling, and cross-country skiing are excellent. Rates are $24 (single) to $32 (double) and include a continental breakfast. If guests prefer not to have breakfast with Jean, lower rates are available. Reservations are suggested.

EM'S BED & BREAKFAST INN

304 Wapato
Chelan, WA
98816
509 682-4149

Marlene Schlittler's intention was to create an environment in which her guests would feel comfortable. She has succeeded. Marlene's turn-of-the-century home is located just a block and a half from beautiful Lake Chelan, where guests can enjoy swimming, fishing, and boating. Or on lazy summer days, guests may instead choose to ease back and relax on the porch swing while they gaze at the lovely panoramic view of the foothills. One of the guest rooms has a fireplace and three of the rooms have queen-size beds. During the evening guests are welcome to curl up in front of the living room fireplace with a good book and let the warmth from the fire bathe their spirits. Breakfast is served in the comfortable dining room. Rates are $40 to $45 for a double, children are welcome, and reservations are suggested.

METCHEE INN

P.O. Box 322A
Winthrop, WA
98862
509 996-2035

Penny and Dan Stuckey have created a slice of Americana complete with rustic log beds and handmade quilts. The inn, which was originally built in 1925, is located in downtown Winthrop. It has two guest rooms downstairs and a small apartment-like unit upstairs with a kitchen and three beds. All accommodations are equipped with television and air conditioning. Guests are welcome in the living room to play chess, enjoy the Steinway concert grand piano, or simply relax. If you're lucky, Penny, who used to be an actress, may play a few melodies on the piano for you. A continental breakfast is made available and is served on the front porch during the summer months. Rates are $35 to $45 for a double and reservations are suggested.

The bed and breakfast industry is beginning to develop east of the Cascade Mountains. Although Central and Eastern Washington have some extraordinary scenery, and Spokane is Washington's second largest city, bed and breakfast travellers will not have to share this area with an abundance of tourists. In this book we have combined most of the central part of the state (excluding Leavenworth, Winthrop, Pateros, and Chelan, which we have placed in the Cascade Mountains chapter) with the eastern portion and labeled it Eastern Washington.

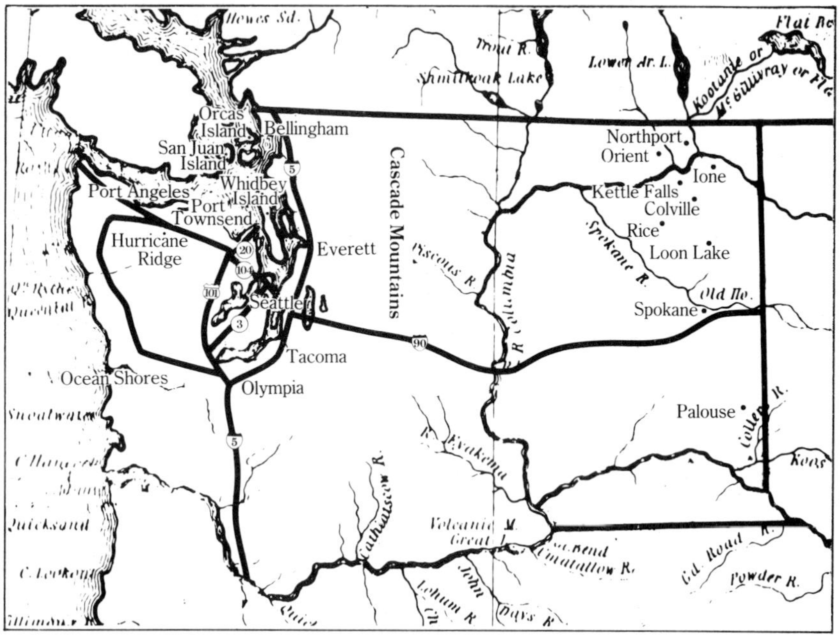

Interstate 90 is the main thoroughfare west to east. From Ellensburg, which is the geographic center of the state and the home of Central Washington State College, east to Spokane, the landscape appears mostly as brown low-rolling hills.

The central part of the state does not offer visitors much in the way of facilities. The land is vast, sparsely populated, and recreational opportunities exist primarily for rugged individuals who love the great outdoors.

With the exception of Grand Coulee Dam, recreational opportunities are near the towns of Ellensburg, Yakima, Wenatchee, and Moses Lake. Fishing, hunting, the rodeo, and tours of Grand Coulee Dam top the list of things to do.

As one nears Spokane, the terrain and recreational opportunities begin to change. This land has been left undiscovered by most vacationers who have tended to stay on the interstate and have shunned the roads leading into the back country. Because of this shyness, they have missed some of the most awesome and beautiful country Washington has to offer.

Northeast Washington from the Grand Coulee Dam north to the Canadian border and east to Idaho is spectacular.

Roosevelt Lake divides Colville National Forest in half. The lake stretches for 130 miles from the dam north toward Canada. It is ideal for scenic cruising, water-skiing, swimming, and fishing.

But the lake is only one of the adventures that awaits the visitor who ventures into this rugged country. Each season is special for those who love the outdoors.

In winter 49° North offers downhill skiers plenty of thrills as they fly down the 1,700-foot-vertical-drop-slope. The area's snow is perfect for cross-country skiers, and there are numerous trails for snowmobilers.

Freshwater fishing tops the agenda in the spring. There are many clear lakes for anglers to try their luck. Fly fishing is a favorite sport in this area as well.

Summer greets hikers, bicyclists, and naturalists to the mountains, lakes, and streams. But water is still the major draw. Sailing, rafting, water-skiing, and diving are the main attractions.

The landscape is ablaze with color in the fall. Animals of all sizes and species dominate the area and attract camera hounds and hunters.

The southeast corner of the state is composed mostly of farmland. The main exception is the Umatilla National Forest, which edges into Washington but is mostly in Oregon. Much of the forest on the Washington side has been preserved as wilderness back-country area. One hundred fifty miles of trails wind their way up, over, and through the Blue Mountains.

Palouse is conveniently close to both Pullman, the home of Washington State University, and Moscow, the site of the University of Idaho. At Washington State visitors should make an effort to tour the Conner Zoological Museum, the Anthropological Museum, and the Museum of Art.

Spokane

Spokane is the largest city between Minneapolis and Seattle. It serves as the gateway to the mountains and lakes of Eastern Washington and to the panhandle of Idaho. The 1980 census credited it with a population of 171,300.

The city and county operate 99 parks, and there are 12 national parks and 15 national forests within a day's drive of Spokane. Manito Park is the pride of the city. Duncan Gardens and the Japanese Garden attract about 100,000 visitors each year.

Nearby Mt. Spokane offers fine Alpine skiing in the winter, and there is ample opportunity for cross-country skiing as well. There are four major ski resorts within two hours of the city.

POINTS OF INTEREST

Colville National Forest
Grand Coulee Dam
Manito Park Spokane
Mt. Spokane U.S. 2 east to 206
Roosevelt Lake
Umatilla National Forest
State 129 south

ADDRESSES

Coulee Dam National
Recreation Area
Coulee Dam, WA 99116

Panorama Land
117 West Astor Street
Colville, WA 99114

Spokane Area Convention and
Visitors Bureau
West 609 Spokane Falls Boulevard
Spokane, WA 99201

COLVILLE

Colville, WA
Panorama: 509 684-4571

Gale and Dusty, a couple of "old car nuts," wish to welcome you to their large brick home that overlooks the Colville Valley. Every spring Dusty and Gale celebrate the opening of their antique car museum. Guests will enjoy looking at the cars and reminiscing about a bygone era. Visitors may also enjoy touring the home's basement, which is adorned with Gale's artwork. Accommodations include a king-size bed, color television, and a shared bathroom. Gale and Dusty hope their guests will join them in the family room for a cup of coffee and conversation. The area offers great hunting and fishing, trail bike riding, snowmobiling, and beautiful scenery. Rates are $25 to $36 and reservations are required. Description Provided By Agency.

COLVILLE

Colville, WA
Panorama: 509 684-4571

This two-bedroom house and the 1,000 acres that surround it can be yours for a day, a week, or longer. Imagine the excitement of walking out your front door, jumping aboard your snowmobile or trail bike, and cruising any of the hundreds of miles of trails that lead you through this breathtaking country. You can hunt, ride, and ski without leaving your own yard. Robert and Barbara provide everything you need for the house to make your visit a comfortable one. Rates are $60 (single) to $80 (double) and reservations are required. Description Provided By Agency.

ORIENT

Orient, WA
Panorama: 509 684-4571

This octagonal log cabin is located only six miles from the Canadian border and overlooks the Kettle River. The spacious upstairs suite has a fireplace, queen-size bed, sauna, private bathroom, sitting area, and an upper deck with a view of the river. There is a smaller downstairs bedroom as well. It also has a private bathroom and a view of the river. Recreational opportunities are abundant and include hiking, river rafting, tubing, and mine exploring in the summer. And in the winter there is cross-country skiing and snowmobiling. Polly is an artist and Elmer is a motorcycle enthusiast. Both are involved in community theater. Rates are $65 for a double and $125 for the suite. Reservations are required.

ORIENT

Orient, WA
Panorama: 509 684-4571

Larry and Jean wish to welcome you to their contemporary home. It is located alongside the Kettle River and is only a few miles from the Canadian border. The nearby Colville National Forest beckons those of you who are hikers, rafters, and cross-country skiers to experience the splendor of this rugged country. The accommodations include two downstairs bedrooms that share a bathroom. Larry and Jean invite you to relax in the living room while warming yourself in front of the fireplace. The home also has an organ that you are welcome to play. If you enjoy chasing the eight ball around, the pool table in the recreation room may offer you a challenge. There are also several private mines nearby that Larry and Jean sometimes tour with their guests. Rates are $35 to $45 for a double and reservations are required.

NORTHPORT

Northport, WA
Panorama: 509 684-4571

This grand old home overlooks both the town of Northport and the mighty Columbia River. It is only a few minutes south of the Canadian border. The spacious home is rustic and adorned with antiques. A private entrance is available for guests. Diane and Charles love meeting people. Diane is fluent in French and is really looking forward to putting it to use. Both Diane and Charles are willing to serve as their guests' guides for either hiking or cross-country skiing. Rates are $28 (single) to $38 (double) and reservations are required. Description Provided By Agency.

KETTLE FALLS

Kettle Falls, WA
Panorama: 509 684-4571

Jan's large two-story home is located in a quiet residential area directly across the street from a private athletic club. It is only five miles from Lake Roosevelt, which offers a tremendous variety of water sports. She has two comfortably furnished rooms available that share a bathroom. Guests are welcome to lounge in the large fenced yard, which has a beautiful flower garden. A continental breakfast is included. Rates are $30 (single) to $50 (double). Reservations are required. Description Provided By Agency.

RICE

Rice, WA
Panorama: 509 684-4571

Both children and pets are welcome to this 1923 farmhouse that is surrounded by mountains and is close to both the Columbia River and Lake Roosevelt. Harv is a retired Spanish and German teacher who is now a pilot for the forest service. Barb is an elementary school teacher. Visitors won't have to travel far to discover recreational opportunities. There are many hills and trails on the property for hikers and sightseers. Horseback riders can also enjoy the 350 acres. Croquet, volleyball, and horseshoes are available. And Harv and Barb invite their guests to bring their three-wheelers and trail bikes along for a jaunt through the countryside. There are two bedrooms that share a bathroom. They are available daily from June 1 to August 31. From April to June and from September to November they are available on weekends. Rates are $28 (single) to $36 (double) and reservations are required.

IONE

Ione, WA
Panorama: 509 684-4571

Jim and Phylis would like to welcome you, your children, and your pets to their contemporary home that is located on the east side of the Pend Oreille River. This scenic area offers guests incredible hunting opportunities, fantastic fishing on the river, and super snowmobiling. And on those lazy sunny afternoons, you may enjoy a leisurely paddle boat ride down the river. The nearby Canadian border, Boundary Dam, and Gardner Caves await your arrival and exploration. Both bedrooms have private entrances and private bathrooms. Jim and Phylis invite you to join them for conversation in their living room, which is dominated by a huge fireplace. Breakfast is served family style or privately. Rates are $25 (single) to $35 (double) and reservations are required. Description Provided By Agency.

IONE

Ione, WA
Panorama: 509 684-4571

Guests will enjoy the rural setting of this home that has a spectacular view of the Pend Oreille River. The home's owners, Milt and Hazel, are gracious and have a wonderful sense of humor. Hazel has her own antique shop and has adorned the home with fine furniture from the past. The home is conveniently located within easy driving distance of the Canadian border and Gardner Caves. The area offers great fishing, hunting, hiking, and snowmobiling. Ione is the home of Del Traphagen, a local snowmobile guide. Rates are $20 (single) to $28 (double) and reservations are required. Description Provided By Agency.

SPOKANE

Spokane, WA
Spokane: 509 924-9229

Mary's home is located on a hill that overlooks the Spokane Valley. The rustic two-story home is surrounded by pine trees and offers a large parking area. Mary invites her guests to enjoy the entire house. Visitors will have no difficulty finding a quiet corner for relaxing in this large home that boasts three fireplaces. It also has a spacious deck that overlooks the private swimming pool, which is great for sunbathing or for cooling off on sultry summer days. When Mary's guests first arrive, she puts them at ease with her friendly manner. She visits with them for a while to learn their needs so that she may provide her guests with personal service. Rates are $25 to $30 and reservations are required. Description Provided By Agency.

SPOKANE

Spokane, WA
Spokane: 509 924-9229

This bright and open contemporary home is located in a rustic setting on a private pond. Bird watchers and other nature lovers will enjoy watching the wildlife that inhabits the area. The bedroom is in a private wing of the home. It is large with twin beds and has its own private bathroom. Guests are welcome to relax in the den. They may also use the washer and dryer. Parks, tennis courts, and shopping are all available nearby. Guests prepare their own breakfast in the home's spacious kitchen. Rates are $25 to $35 and reservations are required. Description Provided By Agency.

SPOKANE

Spokane, WA
Spokane: 509 924-9229

Children are welcome to this home that is conveniently located only three miles from the city center. Jim and June can provide a crib, playpen, and roll-away bed for the little ones. There is also a fenced yard with a sandbox and two well-mannered dogs. Both guest rooms have a private entrance and private bathrooms. There is a small sitting room with a fireplace. A delicious breakfast is prepared by June. Rates are $22 to $30 and reservations are required. Description Provided By Agency.

SPOKANE

Spokane, WA
Spokane: 509 924-9229

This turn-of-the-century home is located close to downtown. It is on a bus line and is only minutes from the interstate. Nestled among the trees, this three-story home is hosted by Virgil and Katie. The guest rooms are light and cheery. Children aged seven and older are welcome. Guests may choose either a large or a small breakfast. German, as well as English, is spoken. Rates are $22 to $30 and reservations are required. Description Provided By Agency.

PALOUSE

Palouse, WA
BABS: 206 733-8642

This is genuinely a unique lodging experience. Susanna and Richard have turned this former grain elevator into a beautiful and comfortable home that is surrounded by rolling fields of wheat. Visitors to either the University of Idaho or Washington State University may find this home an unforgettable experience. Susanna and Richard have two young children, and German, French, and Italian, as well as English, are spoken in the home. Guests may enjoy horseback riding and hiking in the nearby orchards. Home-baked goods and European cuisine are featured. Rates are $18 (single) to $28 (double) and reservations are required. Description Provided By Agency.

LOON LAKE

Loon Lake, WA
Panorama: 509 684-4571

This elegantly furnished home is located within 30 minutes of Spokane in an area that is peppered with lakes. Your hostess, Ida, is an energetic and delightful lady who is an artist. Nearby Loon Lake and Deer Lake are excellent for both fishing and water-skiing. Hunters will discover an abundant variety of game birds in the area. In the winter there is skiing and snowmobiling. Rates are $20 (single) to $36 (double) and reservations are required. Description Provided By Agency.

Washington's Reservation Services

As you already know, many of the homes that are described in this book are listed with a reservation service, or agency. For those homes you must contact their agency to make arrangements for a reservation.

What you may not know is why these homes list with an agency instead of listing independently.

Each of the hosts and hostesses we visited had different reasons for choosing to list their homes in this manner. However, generally these people felt that listing with an agency is more economical (advertising is expensive), less time consuming (someone else is sitting by the phone), and the agency helps to protect the owners' privacy.

In no instance did we find that their reasons had anything to do with the quality or nature of their homes. You will discover that the homes which list with an agency are of the same diverse nature as the homes that are independent.

That being the case, why should you bother to book a reservation through an agency when you could do it directly with an independent home?

The most obvious reason is that the home you have chosen from this book may not be an independent. In order for you to stay there, you must make a reservation through an agency.

Or perhaps you want to stay in several homes in a particular part of the state. In that case the most efficient way to make your reservations is to pick up your telephone and dial the number of an agency in that area. With one phone call you can take care of all your lodging needs.

And bed and breakfast homes are no different than other means of lodging during the tourist seasons. There are a lot of no vacancy signs hanging out front. Some homes are booked months in advance. An agency can help you avoid the frustration of calling several homes just to learn that there is no room in the inn.

Finally, those of you who are not seasoned veterans of travelling the bed and breakfast way may have some fears and concerns about your accommodations or your ability to ask the right questions. An agency can help you by being objective and by booking you into a home that will suit your needs.

When you contact an agency, there are several things that you should look for in the way of service.

First, you should be treated politely. It should be noted that each agency which appears in this book answered my many questions with patience and the utmost courtesy. But if your agent should be discourteous or short with you, hang up and find another agency. If you don't you may not receive the service you need, and you may be very disappointed with your accommodations. Chances are the rude agent doesn't care much about your feelings and will not give you personal service.

When you are talking with the agent, he or she should be willing to spend some time with you asking pertinent questions. It is important that the agent ask you relevant questions in order for you to receive the personal attention you need and deserve.

Some of the questions you should be asked are: Do you smoke? Do you have any special needs? Are your children travelling with you and, if they are, how many are there and how old are they? Are your pets travelling with you? Do you want a private or a shared bathroom? And then there are the obvious questions about desired location, accommodations, length of stay, etc.

Before calling an agency, you should have a list of questions you want answered. And don't be afraid to ask them. Again, if the agency is not willing to attend to every detail and answer your every question, you need to find another agency.

One final point that I believe is important. I don't think there is any substitute for firsthand knowledge. That is why we visited most of the homes in this book, and we told you which ones were not visited. I feel that agencies should visit any home for which they are booking reservations.

Before you make a reservation through an agency, ask the agent if he, she, or someone else in the agency has visited the home. If the answer is no, find out why. Sometimes there just hasn't been enough time because the home is a new listing. In any case, if the home hasn't been visited, find out how the agency gathered their information and how they know that it is accurate.

An important point to keep in mind is that some of you neither need nor desire the services of an agency. You know what you want, where it is, and would prefer to deal directly with the host or hostess of the home. Call your favorite independent and make your own reservation.

You should also realize that the agency normally charges a commission to the host home which is not tacked onto the rates that you pay. You will pay the same whether you book directly through the host home or if you go through an agency.

Homes that are located in heavy tourist regions tend not to list with an agency. The major exception to this in Washington is Seattle. In other tourist areas, if you want to stay in a bed and breakfast home you will probably have to make your own reservations. Check with the agencies for further information about the area you wish to visit.

Following is a list of eight agencies which make reservations for bed and breakfast homes in the state of Washington. A brief description of each one's services is included.

With the exceptions of Bed and Breakfast Port Angeles, Northwest Bed & Breakfast, and PT International (these agencies chose not to share their listings with us), you will find the homes of each agency listed in their respective geographic regions.

We did not include all of the homes that list with Pacific and Travellers'. These are the two largest agencies in the state, and they were gracious enough to give us their complete lists so that we could contact each of their homes for a personal visit. Unfortunately, we ran out of time. We hope to include all of their listings in the next edition. So keep in mind that both of these agencies list more homes, and you should contact Pacific and Travellers' for more information about their homes.

It is also important for you to realize that some of these agencies do book independent homes. And remember that rates are the same whether you make a reservation through an agency or directly with the independent. Call the agencies for further information about which independents they serve.

PACIFIC BED & BREAKFAST

701 N.W. 60th Street
Seattle, WA
98107
206 784-0539

By visiting the homes that list with Pacific, we learned that Irmgard Castleberry's homes are clean, comfortable, and offer excellent service. Irmgard was born and grew up in Germany. She moved to the United States about 20 years ago and has been running a reservation service in Washington since 1981. She is a member of Bed & Breakfast Associated Reservation Services and can help people find agencies in other states. Irmgard has very high standards for her host homes and works closely with hosts and hostesses to make sure these standards remain high. If you choose to call Pacific, Irmgard will do her best to put you in a home that suits your needs. She is a firm believer in personal service.

TRAVELLERS' BED & BREAKFAST

P.O. Box 492
Mercer Island, WA
98040
206 232-2345

On my visits to the homes that list with Travellers', I experienced warm hospitality in clean and comfortable surroundings. Jean Knight began Travellers' in 1981. She was born and grew up in England and came to the United States 14 years ago. Jean visits the homes that list with her, and she makes a sincere effort to ensure compatiblity between guest and host. She is dedicated to providing personal service to prospective guests and is very concerned about maintaining high standards. As well as booking reservations, Jean can also help her guests make arrangements for rental cars and local tours. Travellers' is a member of American Bed & Breakfast Association.

BABS

P.O. Box 5025
Bellingham, WA
98227
206 733-8642

Dolores and George Herrmann wish to make economic travel available to people from all over the world. In order to accomplish this, they don't list any homes that charge more than $30 for a double. "Our hosts are outgoing and interesting people who are more interested in their guests than in making an income from bed and breakfast," George says. BABS' homes are mostly located in Northwest Washington, but they also have listings in Seattle and Eastern Washington.

Prospective guests pay a registration fee of $2.75 plus $1.00 for shipping and handling to receive BABS' guidebook.

PT INTERNATIONAL

1318 S.W. Troy Street
Portland, OR
97219
503 245-0440
or 1 800 547-1463

Clyde Perkins is dedicated to serving the traveller and properly representing the host family or inn. As well as booking a speedy reservation, PTI can assist you with car rentals and itinerary planning. PTI will also provide you with a free brochure that explains their reservation program.

SPOKANE BED AND BREAKFAST

P.O. Box 11103
Spokane, WA
99211
509 924-9229
or 924-0840

Mark Davis runs a real estate firm in Spokane as well as this agency. He has four homes that do bed and breakfast on a regular basis and six others that can handle overflow.

BED AND BREAKFAST PORT ANGELES

139 West 14th
Port Angeles, WA
98362
206 457-3424

Most of the homes that list with Charles and Edith McLeroy do bed and breakfast on a part-time basis. If you are in Port Angeles or are going to Port Angeles and can't find a place to stay, Charles and Edith can probably help you. They have about 25 homes in the Port Angeles area with rates ranging from $30 to $50.

NORTHWEST BED & BREAKFAST

7707 S.W. Locust Street
Portland, OR
97223
503 246-8366

Northwest Bed & Breakfast is a reservation service/membership organization. In order to use the service, prospective guests must first pay a membership fee of $15 a year for singles or $20 a year for a family. Guest members receive a directory which describes each home in Northwest's network. Laine Friedman and Gloria Shaich told us that each home is visited before it is accepted into their network. They insist upon high standards for comfort, cleanliness, and safety.

PANORAMA LAND BED & BREAKFAST

117 West Astor
Colville, WA
99114
509 684-4571

If you're looking for a bed and breakfast home in Northeast Washington, Gail and Jan are the people to contact. They only began their operation in the fall of 1983, but already have many fine homes in and around Colville. Panorama Land can help you with more than bed and breakfast reservations. They can help you plan your entire vacation to this part of the state.

Starting Your Own Bed and Breakfast

by Mark Montgomery

Mark is a bed and breakfast innkeeper and consultant. He and Betsy Montgomery are the co-proprietors of Edel Haus, a bed and breakfast inn in Leavenworth, Washington.

Long before motels came into existence, people were sharing their homes with weary travellers. This tradition has evolved into the present form of bed and breakfast inns. To an ever-increasing number of people, bed and breakfast is the way to go when travelling away from home.

The popularity of bed and breakfast homes has also increased the interest in becoming an innkeeper. Practically every guest who has ever stayed in an inn considers for a moment how wonderful it would be to open a bed and breakfast home. For most people that's as far as they allow their emotions to take them. But for a few, this is just the beginning.

Every so often one of our guests will ask me what I do for a living. They look around at our large house with four rooms for rent and can't imagine what Betsy and I do all day. Like any occupation, the only way to really know what an innkeeper goes through is to try it for yourself. I know of no other job where a person needs to be a cook, a maintenance person, a promotional manager, a secretary, a maid, and a counselor all before noon on any given day. Innkeepers also need to be knowledgeable about insurance, law, accounting, and banking.

How can anyone be properly prepared for all of the crazy predicaments that we innkeepers find ourselves struggling through? We can't. It's impossible to know how to handle an obnoxious, intoxicated guest at 8 a.m. until it happens one morning while you're cooking French toast. There are usually plenty of spectators who are willing to offer advice on such matters. In theory they usually know what to do. But in reality each situation is different and so are the circumstances leading up to it.

Most innkeepers will agree that the best way to handle a problem is to prevent it in the first place. This is why reasonable and firm policies are so important. They allow an innkeeper to prevent most problems by using proven industry standards. For new inns it's wise to follow the policies of established homes until enough experience is gained to evaluate and customize those policies to suit your individual needs.

Many people think that all you have to do to open a bed and breakfast home is to put the extra bed in the guest room, sweep the room out, and hang up a sign. This may be true in other countries but not in the United States. When you start charging money for the use of your home, that portion of the house becomes a place of business. As the owner you are legally responsible for that business. Most of us are aware of the courts these days and how they are overflowing with lawsuits. This is one reason why liability insurance is needed for any business venture. Not only should individuals be personally insured, but corporations or partnerships should be insured also.

As well as liability insurance, you will need other protection. Once a house has been converted to an inn, the value of the building will probably increase. The remodeling, furniture, equipment, and even the business need to be insured in case of theft or fire. Since the house is now a place of business, it should be insured under a business policy. You should be covered for the full replacement value of the inn as well as any loss of business while rebuilding. Don't forget to have your personal items covered. It usually doesn't cost much to include those items in a business policy.

Innkeepers are not the only ones responsible for the general public while they are staying in inns. The city, county, and state are also responsible. It is their job to establish and enforce rules to protect the public. In the state of Washington, lodging facilities with three or more rooms that are booked for less than a month at a time must be licensed as Transient Accommodations by the Department of Social and Health Services. Inns must comply with the health department regulations as well as the fire protection requirements which are enforced by the state fire marshal. These regulations are lengthy and often overwhelming to hopeful innkeepers.

One of the greatest mistakes an innkeeper can make is to purchase a house for conversion to a bed and breakfast home before finding out what it will cost to bring the house up to code.

The Swan Inn, Vashon Island

Converting a house to an inn is expensive and in some cases nearly impossible. To find out exactly what your building will need, you should apply to the state for a Transient Accommodation license. The health inspector and fire marshal will inspect the building and fill out a report which will list the home's deficiencies. The city or county health departments are the ones to contact for food service and hot tub permits.

Next, contact the appropriate contractors and ask them to bid on the necessary remodeling. Be very careful not to make any mistakes on the remodeling project. Be sure to work closely with public officials to prevent any possible misunderstandings. These officials can save you lots of money and frustration if you contact them early in the project. Just imagine what it would feel like to have spent your life savings, quit your job, and borrowed $100,000 on a house just to find out that the windows are too small to keep the license. This is the kind of nightmare that is common to prospective innkeepers.

A good consultant who is familiar with the codes can save you hundreds and sometimes thousands of dollars on your project. Before making commitments of any kind, hopeful innkeepers should analyze the potential inn thoroughly. Keep in mind that bed and breakfast homes are really just small hotels with the same problems as large ones. A complete feasibility study should be done before risking time, money, and your emotional health. The study should include, among other things, projections for room and occupancy rates, fixed expenses, and the amount of capital needed to make the inn a viable business. The study should be done by an objective and experienced consultant.

Before lending money for a business venture, banks usually will require a feasibility study. This is particularly true for an inn. Bank loan officers realize that emotions play a big role with innkeepers and that emotions have a way of distorting reality.

After the feasibility study is completed, you should look at it closely and consider if the return on your investment is going to suit your financial needs. Very few innkeepers ever receive the salary that was planned on. But there are other benefits.

Most of us live in a home that we could not otherwise afford, and we have a lifestyle unlike any other. There are also some very good tax benefits to take advantage of. Since almost everything we spend money on is a business expense, there is very little net taxable income. Most innkeepers choose to reinvest any extra money back into the inn instead of taking a salary that is taxable. Many consider their equity in the inn a retirement income for the future that can be drawn upon when the inn is sold. This gives innkeepers an extra incentive to establish an inn that is popular. If the occupancy rate is high, the inn will be worth more, and the retirement benefits will be greater.

Opinions vary dramatically on how to create a popular inn. However, there are some basic principles that are commonly used in most successful inns. All rooms that are used by guests are thoroughly cleaned and refreshed after every use. Bathrooms, whether private or shared, are used only by guests in the assigned rooms. Innkeepers, employees, and nonpaying visitors do not share bathrooms with guests. Breakfast is made of the freshest ingredients available with a great deal of emphasis on nutrition and taste. These are the minimum standards that inn travellers expect. Very few will accept anything less.

What really brings guests back time and time again? Usually it's the personal touches and friendships that provide us all with fond memories. Fresh-cut flowers and a genuine smile go a long way in making a guest's stay enjoyable. Many of our guests at the Edel Haus have left or sent us small gifts and thank-you cards. These thank you's are extremely rewarding. We look forward to our returning guests because they are accustomed to our home, and it proves to us that they really enjoy what we have to offer. This gives us a sense of accomplishment. We also realize that if our guests enjoy themselves, they will encourage their friends and family to visit us too. Word-of-mouth advertising is the backbone of most inns. You need to pay close attention to your referrals and returning guests. If after 18 months of operation the number of returning guests is less than 20% of your business, you either have a serious problem or an endless supply of first-time guests.

A good reputation is vital for a bed and breakfast home, but without excellent promotion no one will ever find out about your inn in the first place. Newspapers, magazines, and television have given extensive coverage to homes. This kind of advertising is fast, effective, and free. Small inns can't afford a lot of paid advertising. So free advertising is very important. Books are also a good source of advertising. They are usually kept longer than newspapers and magazines, so the benefits could last for years.

If you are opening an inn, you should write personal letters to travel editors and authors to be certain that they find out about your inn. The letter should describe the character of the inn and important or interesting historical data. The letter should also cover your background and the reasons why you decided to become an innkeeper.

Sally's, Langley

You might think that word-of-mouth, articles about your business in newspapers and magazines, and being listed in books and associations would be enough exposure for a small inn. But even inns with a good location and high visibility usually need to buy some advertising. Buying effective advertising for inns is challenging. It can also be expensive. Sometimes it is possible to save money on advertising by joining with several other homes in your area and purchasing group advertising.

Other than advertising through the media, an attractive and informative brochure is the innkeeper's best promotional tool. As well as being informative, the brochure should accurately portray an image of the inn and act as a lure. It can be distributed to travel agents, chamber of commerce offices, and anywhere else you think it may do some good. A few brochures in the hands of a happy guest will undoubtedly produce some good results.

Like other professionals, a good innkeeper will make his or her job look easy. But the pressure on an innkeeper can be severe and quite complicated. It is not uncommon for an owner of a bed and breakfast home to work an entire season without a day off. This is especially true at first when you are trying to establish a good reputation. After a year or two, the stress of long hours and little pay will get to almost anyone. Most innkeepers experience "burnout" at some point in the first few years of operation. It is not a popular subject with hopeful innkeepers, but it is extremely important to keep in mind. Steps must be taken to avoid this unfortunate problem. Days off, plenty of rest, and occasional vacations are a must in order to stay fresh and happy. Physical and mental health should top the priorities of an innkeeper. A bed and breakfast is a very personal business, so if the innkeeper is healthy and happy it will be reflected in the inn.

There are many things to consider when opening an inn, most of which can be worked out through determination and an ample supply of common sense. If you are one of the many people considering turning your existing home into an inn or purchasing another home with that thought in mind, it may be best to begin with just one or two bedrooms. This can provide a good second income without the great expense of extensive remodeling.

Remember, the state only requires inns with three or more rooms to be licensed as Transient Accommodations. Some counties are also adopting rules governing small inns, but their codes are usually not as strict as the state's. Starting small enables you to begin slowly without making a long-term commitment. You will soon discover whether or not being an innkeeper is right for you. If it isn't, you have lost nothing and perhaps gained some new friends.

No matter what size inn you decide to begin with, remember that it is a business and must be run that way in order to have a chance for success. Running a bed and breakfast home is not for everyone. But for those who can appreciate the business, I can think of nothing better.

Acknowledgements

We wish to express our sincere gratitude to the proprietors of Washington's bed and breakfast homes who gave us so much of their precious time. We also wish to give special thanks to Irmgard Castleberry and Jean Knight, who helped us get the project started in the right direction. Our gratitude is extended to the Department of Commerce & Economic Development for providing us with much needed information. And finally, our heartfelt thanks to Lucille and Frank Kuechenmeister, who were there when we needed them.